The Garden at Larnach Castle

The Garden at Larnach Castle

MARGARET BARKER

Published 2006 by David Bateman Ltd,
Unit 2/5 Workspace Drive, Hobsonville, New Zealand
Reprinted 2019

ISBN: 978-1-98-853809-9

Project manager, editor: Sarah Beresford
Designed by Janis Ord, Jazz Graphics
Printed in China through Colorcraft Ltd, Hong Kong

TITLE PAGE: *A doorway frames a moonlight maple (*Acer shirasawanum *'Aureum' syn* A. japonicum*).*
PREVIOUS SPREAD: *On occasion the garden disappears beneath a blanket of snow.*
ABOVE: *New Zealand's iconic cabbage trees (*Cordyline australis*) are clustered at the Castle entrance.*
FOLLOWING PAGE: *Azaleas aflame before the Castle.*

Margaret Barker with her son Norcombe, her daughter Sophie's child Charlotte, Fern and Sophie.

Acknowledgements

NO BOOK IS AN ISLAND and I would like to thank the many people who helped with this project. Fiona Eadie, the Castle head gardener, corrected the botanical nomenclature and helped sort the photographs and also the captions. Deborah Raffills read the text and made suggestions, as did my children Sophie and Norcombe Barker. Peter Arthur, Jim Guest and Kathryn Millar commented on the text.

Tracy MacAulay typed most of the script, transcribing my horrible handwriting. Paula Booth entered the corrections to the final draft.

There were other people who helped me with hospitality, friendship and encouragement, enabling me to get on with the job of writing. These included Ian and Rosie Morten, who hosted me on a writer's retreat, Judy McIlwraith, Fleur Snedden, Eve Nicholas, Beverley McConnell, Liz Morrow and Robyn Kilty. Fiona Curd advised on the traditional meaning of the koru to Maori. Brian and Michael Seatter coped with technical issues with discs.

Gordon Collier kindly offered to proofread the text. Tracey Borgfeldt, associate publisher at David Bateman Ltd, has been enormously supportive from first receiving the outline for this book. Sarah Beresford as editor and Janis Ord, the designer, have together created this delightfully presented book from what was assuredly an enormous mass of disparate material. It was Neil Ross who first suggested that I write this book when he saw my presentation at the Ellerslie Flower Show in 2004.

None of this would have been possible had it not been for the inspirational photography of Stephen Jaquiery, and the additional photographs by his wife Jane Dawber, which recorded the garden and its happenings over two years. His photography has also captured the Otago Peninsula in its many moods. An Antarctic gale kicked the helicopter around as he took the superb aerial photograph of the Castle in the snow. Without these images the Ellerslie talk would not have been possible, nor would there be this book. Gil Hanly, one of New Zealand's most experienced garden photographers, has also created some wonderful images. Others who have supplied photographs are Barry Barker, Juliet Nicholas, Sally Tagg, Allied Press, John Murray, Andris Apse, Lindsay McLeod, Moira Clark, Stewart Preston, Deborah Raffills, Darea Sheratt, Tourism Dunedin, and Anne-Marie Mains. Zuna Wright painted the garden map.

Many off the staff at Larnach Castle have helped in different ways and in particular I would like to thank the gardeners both past and present because without gardeners there would be no garden.

Margaret Barker
March 2006

PAGE FOLLOWING CONTENTS: *The Cupola, which once graced the saloon of the sailing ship Zealandia, was installed at the Castle in 1927. Oamaru stone urns on the right mark the entrance to the Serpentine Walk.*

Contents

PROLOGUE.................. PAGE 16
February 1967

CHAPTER 1.................. PAGE 20
A Bite of History

CHAPTER 2.................. PAGE 28
Early Years

CHAPTER 3.................. PAGE 38
The Lost Rock Garden

CHAPTER 4.................. PAGE 50
The Serpentine Walk

CHAPTER 5.................. PAGE 60
A Step Out from the Ballroom

CHAPTER 6.................. PAGE 70
Slowly, Slowly I Find My Way

CHAPTER 7 .... PAGE 80

A New Vision

CHAPTER 8 .... PAGE 90

Achieving Clarity

CHAPTER 9 .... PAGE 102

Dare I Mention My Love Affair with Rhododendrons?

CHAPTER 10 .... PAGE 112

South Seas Garden

CHAPTER 11 .... PAGE 126

Southern Plants from Southern Lands

CHAPTER 12 .... PAGE 140

Now This Is the Garden

HOT TIPS .... PAGE 148

From the Gardeners at Larnach Castle

VISITOR INFORMATION .... PAGE 154

SELECTED BIBLIOGRAPHY ...... PAGE 156

PHOTOGRAPHIC CREDITS ..... PAGE 157

INDEX .... PAGE 158

PARK

PROLOGUE

February 1967

We ventured down the dark drive. Towering trees met overhead. My husband Barry and I were on holiday touring the South Island, and sleeping in the back of our panel van. We lived in Wellington, had been married for just a year, and were expecting our first baby. We were searching for a legendary Castle which, we were told, was on a 300-metre hill on the remote Otago Peninsula. The tangle of overgrowth opened out and suddenly it was before us, Larnach Castle, dreaming in the summer sun of lost days of grandeur.

We paid our admission at the door to Oscar Empson, and explored innumerable empty rooms. Vast sunlit verandas were flecked with rich colours – blue, green, red and amber light shone through the Venetian glass windows. Then we entered the shadowed inner foyer, with its astounding richly carved ceiling.

When it was closing time, we reluctantly prepared to leave. "I wish it were mine," Barry said to Oscar on the front doorstep.

"You can have it," Oscar replied. With a certain excitement, Barry and I were discussing the possibilities when a voice echoed down the hall.

"But Oscar it's sold." The voice belonged to Clarissa, Oscar's bedridden wife and the owner of the Castle. Yes, it was sold, but the buyers had failed to pay the deposit.

Anxious to sell because of Clarissa's failing health, Oscar showed us some of the locked rooms.

As we descended stone steps to an underground cellar, Barry shared a secret with Oscar: "My wife's having a baby."

"That's obvious," Oscar replied.

This is the Castle as I first saw it in 1967. It changed my life.

In one of the bedrooms, Oscar picked up a hat decorated with flowers and ribbons. "Clarissa bought this to wear to a wedding, but she will never wear it now," he said as he sadly put it down.

Their tenure was ending. Was ours about to begin?

As evening came, the Castle was enveloped in impenetrable mist. Barry and Oscar shared a few brandies.

The next day I went to the land transfer office and searched the title. Was it really true that we could buy what we perceived as a treasure? We went to see the lawyers handling the transaction and they assured us that, yes, we could. At that time the Castle was locally disregarded, its crumbling structure a sad reminder of misplaced ambitions.

"Oh that old place – it's falling down, isn't it?" we were to hear, time and time again. We had to make our own assessment of its significance and potential.

We were aware of some of the Castle's many problems. It was evident that when it rained, water poured in. Graffiti was carved into the Oamaru stone battlements of the tower and the plaster walls on the top floor and the ceilings of the two upper storeys had gaping holes. The integrity of the joists was in question, although the structural stone appeared in good order. The Empsons had opened the building to the public on an intermittent basis, but for their own reasons declined to give us any indication of the income they received from this.

There were many unknowns. A purchase would be a leap of faith. Barry had for several years been a member of the Travel and Holidays Association, now the Tourist Industry Association. He perceived that tourism would be New Zealand's growth industry and saw in the Castle an opportunity to enter this field.

I was influenced by my parents and childhood. My mother had created a garden. My sister, brother and I as children ran free in our own and other large gardens on Napier's Bluff Hill. I wanted the same for our children – I pictured them making huts, running free, being aware of the processes of nature.

After serving in World War I, my father studied music on a scholarship at the Paris Conservatoire. The education included architecture, his teacher explaining that music and architectural composition were one. My father kept hundreds of annotated postcards of English and European buildings that

CLOCKWISE, FROM TOP LEFT: *The entrance gate to the castle as it looked in 1967. Margaret and Barry with their car, 'the yellow submarine'. The Lost Rock Garden. The state of things behind the Castle. The New Zealand Divisional Orchestra of the original Kiwi Concert Party taken about 1917. My father is the flautist seated in the centre row, second from right. The Raised Lawn looking towards what is now a hedge with the car park and beech trees beyond.*

he had known. From him I inherited my love of old buildings. In Larnach Castle, I saw the aspirations and confidence of a colonial founder in this new land.

Restoring the Castle and making it our home would be both a vocation and an adventure. We dreamt that one day it would be carefully furnished and set in a beautiful garden, becoming a symbol of our colonial history.

We made up our minds to buy. My decision was intuitive. At 24, you don't think things through and I felt empowered by the challenge.

We went back to Wellington to wind up our affairs and Barry organised the finance for the purchase of the Castle. A fortnight later, we drove onto the Inter-Island ferry to make the overnight journey from Wellington to Lyttelton in our yellow Studebaker Coupe. We called it the 'yellow submarine' after the Beatles' song. We had thrown all the last minute things to pack into the back of the car – pots, pans and pillows. A removal firm had already taken south the large items. We left behind our life in Wellington.

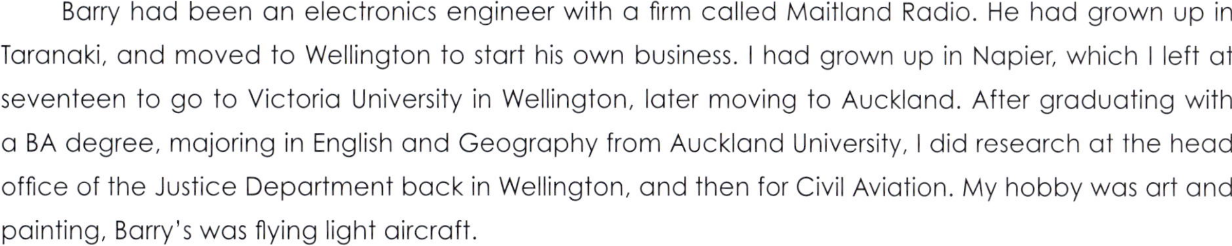

Barry had been an electronics engineer with a firm called Maitland Radio. He had grown up in Taranaki, and moved to Wellington to start his own business. I had grown up in Napier, which I left at seventeen to go to Victoria University in Wellington, later moving to Auckland. After graduating with a BA degree, majoring in English and Geography from Auckland University, I did research at the head office of the Justice Department back in Wellington, and then for Civil Aviation. My hobby was art and painting, Barry's was flying light aircraft.

From Lyttelton we drove south over the Canterbury Plains. We had to complete the deal for the purchase of the Castle by 2.30pm that day. It was before the days of telegraphic transfers, so we had the money with us in a bag, in the form of a bank draft. Just south of Ashburton the car got a flat tyre. Where was the jack? In the boot of course, under the pots, pans and pillows. We took these out and spread them around on the side of the road. With our few possessions, and with me heavily pregnant, Barry and I looked like refugees. The jack would not fit under the chassis as the back of the car was still overloaded with kitchen, bedding and bathroom ware. We had to decide whether to dig a hole for the jack in the side of the road or completely unload the car.

It was a typically hot Canterbury summer day. We were ever mindful that we had to get the money in the bag to Dunedin by 2.30pm sharp. Fortunately, some farmers saw our plight, stopped, lent us their jack and helped us change the tyre. We were on our way.

We arrived on time, completed the sale and moved into the Castle. We made up a bed in the master bedroom, on the second floor, with its view of the ruined garden. On 4 March 1967, my twenty-fifth birthday, I awoke to a new life at Larnach Castle.

CHAPTER ONE

A Bite of History

Aotearoa, the Land of the Long White Cloud, was settled by Maori perhaps a thousand years ago. Brilliant navigators, they sailed from their Pacific islands to the north in long canoes, or waka. Some came to the south of the country and lived around the coast of Otago, which was the Maori name for the harbour. Captain James Cook sailed by in 1770 and named Mt Charles on the Otago Peninsula. In the early nineteenth century whalers and sealers made a base on the peninsula and a few Europeans settled to service the passing ships.

Sailors and escaped convicts from Australia brought European diseases, including syphilis and measles, to the area. Maori had no resistance to these diseases and their population suddenly declined. Two shiploads of English and Scottish members of the Free Church of Scotland arrived to colonise Dunedin in 1848. 'Dunedin' was the Gaelic name for Edinburgh. Life was hard, with farming expanding only gradually and progress was limited by a shortage of capital.

Gold was discovered in Gabriels Gully in Otago in 1861. This glittering prize was found elsewhere in inland Otago and suddenly the rush was on. Dunedin was the provincial capital but at that time was just a struggling wooden village with clay streets which in winter were ankle deep in mud. Overnight it became a cosmopolitan boom town. Lured by the promise of instant wealth, prospectors came from the goldfields of Victoria in Australia and California in the United States. In their wake came the camp followers – the thieves, ruffians, entertainers, publicans, harlots, traders, merchants and, inevitably, bankers.

The Castle and surrounding countryside as painted in 1889 by J. S. Willis.

Into this scene stepped an Australian banker from New South Wales, William Larnach. The son of a landowner who had emigrated to Australia from Scotland, Larnach had most recently managed the Bank of New South Wales in Geelong. When he was 24 he had managed a bank in a tent on the goldfields of Ararat where his 'office furniture' consisted of strong boxes, dogs and guns. Larnach had travelled to London in 1866, where he and his wife Eliza and their four children stayed with his uncle, Sir Donald Larnach, at 21 Kensington Palace Gardens. Donald Larnach was London manager of the Bank of New South Wales and introduced his nephew to influential bankers, including the Rothschilds and the Barings. Donald also influenced William Larnach, kindling his desire to one day own an elegant estate.

As a result of his new contacts, Larnach was appointed by the bank's London directors as chief colonial manager of the Bank of Otago in Dunedin. Larnach arrived in 1868 and opened thirteen branches for the Bank of Otago, but also traded on the side as a supplier to prospectors. He had discovered in the goldfields of Australia that it was the middleman who made the money. He resigned from the Bank of Otago when it merged with the National Bank, and became a merchant, timber miller, landowner, speculator and politician. On the rising tide of gold that flowed through Dunedin, Larnach became a man of great wealth.

One day, when out walking high on Otago Peninsula with his nine-year-old son Donald, Larnach came upon a site with a beautiful view. He decided that this was where he would realise his dream of building a most splendid mansion, such as had never been seen before in the colonies. Plans for the Castle were drawn up by R.A. Lawson, a Scottish architect who had emigrated to Australia and then come to Dunedin when he won the prize to design 'First Church'. It is thought that Larnach and Lawson worked closely together on the design of the mansion.

When Larnach bought the land in 1870 it was covered in bush, including kowhai and broadleaf forest, with large rimu, totara and matai. Larnach had the bush felled and the land cleared. The hilltop, which had been a volcanic fumerole with a solid core of igneous rock at its centre, was lowered 10 metres to create a level site. Larnach Castle was built of stone in the northern European Gothic Revival style, but the traditional architecture underwent a sea change going from the old world to the new. The ground and first floors were enveloped in delicate cast-iron lace verandas. Colonial verandas signalled a more relaxed style of life in a warmer climate with brighter light.

The stone was quarried locally but the decorative materials and embellishments were brought by sailing ships from around the world. These were landed at Port Chalmers, loaded onto punts and taken across the harbour to Broad Bay, and then hauled up the 300-metre hill on oxen-drawn sleds. There were 20 tonnes of glass from France, red, black and white marble from Italy, slate from Wales, ceramics from Stoke-on-Trent and precious woods from every continent. These included English oak, Douglas fir, mahogany, cedar, teak, Tasmanian blackwood, Huon pine, ash and ebony, as well as the local kauri, rimu and rewarewa. Skilled artisans – stonemasons from Scotland, plasterers from Italy, carpenters and brilliant woodcarvers from England – worked together on this isolated site to create a Castle in this far-flung land, so remote from the culture from which it was generated.

With the native forest cleared, the hilltop site was exposed to extreme winds from the Southern Ocean. So the open verandas of the Castle were glassed in and Larnach hurriedly established 40-metre-wide shelter belts. He planted native and exotic trees, including Douglas fir, macrocarpa, Monterey pine, totara, Tasmanian blackwood, oak, poplar, walnut, Tasmanian gums, Norway pine and Scottish maple, cabbage trees, rimu and beech. Monkey puzzle trees were planted as specimens, their reptilian foliage appealing to florid Victorian tastes. Within the garden he created a framework of hedges of holly, laurel and box.

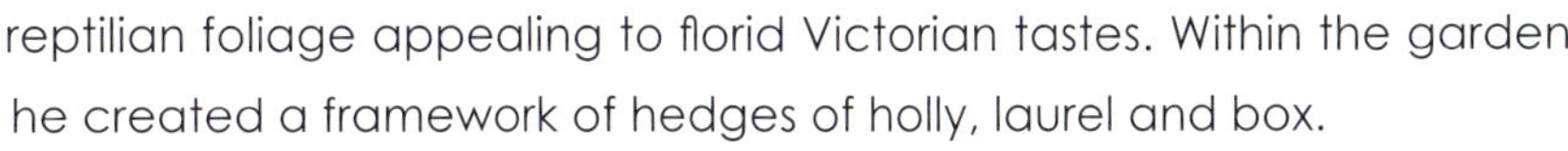

Larnach had a collection of more than 50 ferns which were housed in a glass fernery attached to the Castle's ballroom. There were latticed tunnels of lath, over which grew roses and ivy under-planted with Larnach's favourite flower, the foxglove. A paddock called the 'stars and stripes field' was planted in trees to represent the American flag.

Larnach practised self-sufficiency, as did all large farms of the time. Vegetables were grown, poultry kept for meat and eggs, cows were milked, and butter was made in the dairy. Stone fruit and grapes were ripened in glasshouses and raspberries and strawberries were grown outside. Oats were cropped to feed the horses that provided Larnach's dashing transport into town. He kept twelve carriage horses, six blacks and six greys, which were all bloodstock. Draught horses drew the farm machinery. Larnach had a splendid stable for his horses, their equipment and staff; the grooms slept upstairs in the loft. The stable floor, laid with cobbles shipped from Marseilles in France, was of such quality that it is still in perfect condition. The structural and decorative ironwork was shipped from Glasgow. There was a forge house, where the resident blacksmith shod the horses and kept the farm machinery in good repair. Fencing was post-and-rail, although Larnach increasingly used wire, which was a new idea at that time. Drystone retaining and field walls were built by Scottish stonemasons, although Larnach also enjoyed building these himself, often staying out quite late in the evening to do so.

OPPOSITE: *William Larnach. Larnach Castle in the summer of 1874–5.*
ABOVE LEFT: *Larnach relaxes with family and friends in the lath pergola.* ABOVE: *Guests arrive at the Castle.*

Today these are an enduring feature of the Castle property and the higher peninsula landscape.

Early in our tenure, an elderly visitor explained the mysteries of the three-roomed crenellated building which Larnach had centrally placed at the back of the Castle.

"It was the privy," he told us. "An eight-holer, very posh, complete with brass ashtrays."

In each of the rooms was a wooden seat with two big holes for grown-ups and two smaller holes for children. Contents of the long-drop cans tipped into a chamber below where horse manure, which had been piped underground from the stable nearby, was also collected. The resulting methane gas from this brew was mixed with acetylene gas in a big glass bubble. A gas generator was housed in the central room, and the gas sent underground in lead pipes to the Castle to light the crystal chandeliers.

ABOVE: *The Castle in the first decade of the twentieth century. Macrocarpa shelter trees on what is now the Raised Lawn had grown so large that they were beginning to enclose the Castle.*
RIGHT: *The structure which once housed the methane plant and privy.*

Because methane gas was heavier than air, it had to be pumped up by using a foot pump.

The elderly visitor who told us this tale had long ago been the boy who worked the foot pump. The underground tank was emptied through a trapdoor down the hill and the contents used as compost.

"There were technical difficulties sometimes," he said. "An explosion of gas in the library once blew out all the windows."

Larnach had other homes in Dunedin, Melbourne, Wellington and London and his busy life in politics and business kept him away from the Castle much of the time. His first wife, Eliza, found the Castle too cold and too far from town, preferring to live in Dunedin. Five of his six children were educated overseas.

Larnach's family life was marked by sadness, as he was predeceased by his first two wives and his eldest daughter, Kate. As the gold ran out, the tide of wealth turned to a depression. In the 1890s Larnach's speculations brought him financial grief, and he was personally betrayed by his young third wife and second son. On the 12 October 1898, Larnach took his own life with a single gun shot, while locked in committee room J of New Zealand's House of Parliament.

Larnach died intestate. His younger son and a daughter fought the other three children in court for what remained of Larnach's estate. The Castle was put up for auction in 1900, but failed to reach the reserve. The contents and furniture were sold separately, as were the livestock, farm implements and carriages. In 1906 the government bought the now empty Castle and used it as a mental hospital until 1918, when the patients were moved out to Seacliff, on the coast north of Dunedin.

The government abandoned the Castle and a Mr Nhyon, who owned and lived at the home farm on Camp Road a distance below the Castle, acted as occasional caretaker. Ivan Mitchell, who was once a travel agent in Dunedin, remembers as a little boy looking for an adventure with some other lads and daring to go inside the abandoned property. The black-bearded Mr Nhyon came upon them. There was a ring of pits that surrounded the Castle and Mr Nhyon told them that this was where they threw naughty boys. With terror in their hearts they fled. The Castle slumbered on. The trees that Larnach had planted grew untended and enveloped the Castle, its outbuildings and garden.

In 1927 the Castle was bought by Mr J. Jackson Purdie. His late wife, Laura Purdie, told me that when Mr Purdie was little, he had lived at Port Chalmers. He would look across the harbour at the light of the setting sun reflected from the glass of the Castle. He decided as a boy that one day the Castle would be his. Purdie was a wood and coal merchant in Dunedin and once he had acquired ownership, he felled the trees in the castle grounds and sold the timber. All except for a few specimens and essential shelter fell victim, so that he realised more from the sale of the wood than he had paid for the Castle.

The neglected buildings were restored and electricity was installed. Mr and Mrs Purdie, and both their mothers, moved in and the Castle began a new heyday. Mrs Purdie was both enthusiastic and

knowledgeable about antiques and provided the Castle with marvellous furniture and china, mostly from England and Europe. She was also a gardener, and had the garden laid out in the Victorian style. There was a fernery with trick plumbing which squirted the unknowing visitor with water, patterned beds for annuals, a croquet lawn and a shrubbery behind the ballroom, edged with dwarf box and colourful ribbons of double primroses.

The layout of the Raised Lawn in front of the Castle was Italian in inspiration. Paths with urns each side quartered the lawn and led to a round central pool. Giving focus and sparkle to the pool was a marble fountain which the Purdies had bought in Pisa while on a visit to Italy. They had left instructions for it to be shipped back to New Zealand but it never arrived. Years later, a friend of theirs found a huge parcel in a Sydney warehouse addressed to the Purdies which turned out to be the missing Italian fountain. It was retrieved and installed.

Mrs Purdie bought the glass Cupola, now on the lawn to the left of the Castle, which had been the dome of the saloon from the sailing ship *Zealandia*, salvaged after the ship broke up on the Otago Harbour heads in 1927. She had it mounted on cast-iron posts which were recycled from a shop veranda.

The ball at the top was from the Castle roof and can be seen in old photographs that show a ball on each corner. Decorative work on the glass involved acid etching, enamelling and silver oxide staining which created the yellow and gold. This Art Nouveau tribute to the opium poppy is at its most beautiful when the sun is low and shining through the glass with slanting rays. Then the Cupola glows from within, with a golden light.

The glass dome, when still part of the sailing ship, was perhaps the last thing my own great-grandfather ever saw. He was William Tayler Smith and he travelled aboard the *Zealandia* in September 1902. He carried a large sum of money with which to buy a team of horses. He boarded the boat in Napier on his way to Auckland, but never got off. Neither he nor the money were seen again.

Creating the garden must have been difficult for Mrs Purdie. She told me that she tried to save a special tree and rushed outside, getting her best silk dress in a mess. But she was too late and the tree was felled. A person who had worked in the garden told us that he went to Mr Purdie and told him that he wouldn't take orders from a woman. Her niece, now Mrs Horman, as a child often stayed at the Castle and her task was to clear the leaves out of the little stream in the rock garden.

The Purdie's achievement was that they turned the Castle and gardens into a famous showplace. They opened their home to the paying public for two afternoons a week. Then Mr Purdie contracted Parkinson's disease.

"He got stubborn," Mrs Purdie told me, and although they had a driver, he insisted on driving himself. She was concerned that he would drive off the high peninsula road and roll the car 330 metres down into the sea. Regretfully, they sold the Castle. The building and contents were auctioned separately in 1939 and once more the Castle's furnishings were scattered.

There were a number of subsequent owners over the next 30 years. During World War II, soldiers of

the Signal Corps were billeted here. The Castle remained empty of furniture and was again abandoned during the 1950s. Lead was stolen from the Castle's roof so that water poured in, bringing down the plaster ceilings.

The Castle slipped into general disrepair. Falling cedar branches broke the glass in the Cupola. A giant macrocarpa tree fell on the stable, gashing the roof and letting in the rain. The interior timbers of the stable decayed and, by the time we came, a Douglas fir seedling was growing in the roof. An arsonist had set alight the tangle of dried growth in the vinery and burnt the structure down.

The omnipresent shelter belt had enlarged its territory. Self-sown pines and macrocarpa invaded the garden. Thickets of ponticum rhododendron, berberis, blackberry, sycamore trees and holly crept up to the Castle walls. For a second time the garden was engulfed, but maybe a garden has a reason for being. It called to me for its rescue.

OPPOSITE: *A view of the circular Raised Lawn from the Castle's front door as it was in the 1930s.*
ABOVE: *The Cupola is a tribute in glass to the opium poppy.*

CHAPTER TWO

Early Years

We had big dreams but were yet to grasp the reality. The Castle roof was shot, essential services were unreliable, floors unstable and the empty rooms had the accumulation of 30 years of neglect. Outside were ruined outbuildings, all enclosed by burgeoning, uncontrolled, menacing growth that was eagerly reclaiming its territory. It was bitterly cold and damp – inside – and we had a baby on the way.

Our plump little girl, Sophie, was born in April, six weeks after we arrived. We were ready to take on our challenge. It was a bit like camping. We hadn't much furniture. Often we had no electrical power because the faulty and elderly switchboard failed, or because a tree fell on the mains, so I learnt to manage with kerosene lamps. I would cook on the coal-fired heater in our living room on the first floor, which had once been the Larnach's elaborate breakfast room.

Fixing the roof was a massive problem. Slates had slipped and cracked, lead had been stolen from the tower and replaced with flat galvanised iron which was improperly

ABOVE: *On the steps of the Castle with my parents Helen and Cedric White and baby Sophie.* RIGHT: *Norcombe and Sophie playing by the wishing well. The plant frame bases on the right have gone and the glass vinery has been restored and is now used as a shade house. The dungeon is in the background on the left. The power lines visible on the right have been put underground allowing the decapitated totara tree to grow.*

THE

and, when carrying the baby up to our bedroom at night, I had to sit and rest on the stairs. Someone told my mother of my plight and she flew down and did the washing and generally helped. She thought it best that I have a break, so she arranged for me and my babies to stay on my uncle's farm near Ashburton.

I conscientiously returned to the Castle too soon and was still not strong. Summer staff were living in and I was expected to cook their meals. There were three adults in the family, not a good number, my husband, his mother, and me. My mother-in-law made me feel that everything I did was wrong. There were competing demands from my husband and my babies and I wondered when, in the distant future, my body would again be my own. Because I did not drive a car, I was isolated in the Castle. I had letters from my friends who were enjoying their OE in the swinging London of the 1960s and I thought to myself, 'What on earth am I doing here?'

As the children grew and my physical strength returned, I refocused on what was around me. There was a Castle to restore and furnish, a business to develop and a future garden to dream on. Nights were spent on restoration projects after the children had gone to bed. Working late one night removing inappropriate paint from beautiful woodwork, I felt tired and sat down to rest – in the tray of paint stripper. I got up again in a heck of a hurry and made for a washbasin of water.

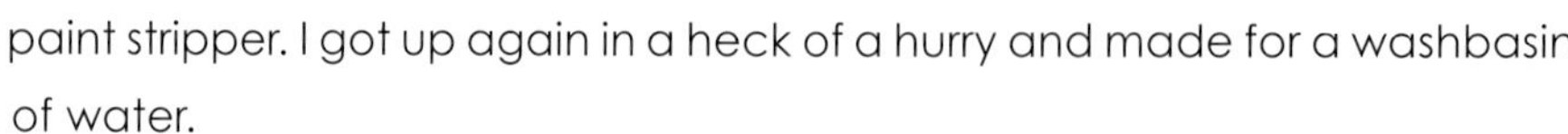

It took years of what can only be described as toil to get the Castle cleaned up and in working order. I only had little bits of time around the edges of my days to go out into the garden. But I read books at night and in my imagination I visited the great gardens of the world.

My mentor in those early years was Mrs Purdie, the chatelaine of the Castle during the 1930s. In years past, she had refused to visit, appalled by the incompetence of subsequent owners and abject at seeing her cherished former home falling into disrepair. But she accepted my invitation to tea. A valued friendship was formed, despite an age difference of nearly 60 years. We had the best interests of the Castle at heart. Mrs Purdie's uncle had been a friend of Larnach's and he had given her information about its history. When she lived at the Castle, she had entertained some of the Larnach's surviving servants, who told her of life at the Castle then and of the running of the household, and Mrs Purdie passed on this oral history to me.

With this knowledge, and by letting the rooms speak to me, I gradually assembled furnishings of the period from 1870 to 1900. Where possible, original items were located and brought home and the search was constant. Otherwise, I mainly collected items made of New Zealand indigenous woods. This took time. There was a shortage of money, and restoration of the building itself took priority. I often waited years to put in place exactly what was right for a particular room. Even now, pieces of the jig-saw come to light. These authentic items tell the tale of how people lived in this home long ago.

Mrs Purdie told me that she had acquired the signal cannon from Taiaroa Head and had placed it under the Cupola at the side of the house. Before the days of radio, this cannon had been fired when a ship was sited off Taiaroa Head to alert those in the harbour at Port Chalmers. The Purdies went

to America in 1939, leaving caretakers in charge of the Castle. When they returned the cannon was missing. When Mrs Purdie enquired, the caretakers admitted that when they had held a party, one of the guests had chucked the cannon down the wishing well. Thirty years later we lowered a tall thin lad down the eight-metre well and he was intrigued to help us retrieve the cannon. We now have this little item of Otago Harbour history, which has had its ups and downs, displayed inside the Castle.

At that time there were still people who could share personal memories of Larnach himself. A lady in her nineties told me that she went with her father to see Larnach come out on the balcony of the hotel at Lawrence after he had been re-elected as Member of Parliament for Tuapeka in 1894. He was so drunk that he had to be held up by his daughters on each side. One of them took off his hat and waved it to the crowd.

She told me that Larnach had a cock pit. Larnach and his political and business friends took part in the illegal sport of cock fighting somewhat furtively in a hidden, gated area. Ladies were not allowed to watch as the spurred cocks fought to the death. My sprightly informant said that her father bred the birds and before a fight they were polished with silk handkerchiefs. I phoned Mrs Purdie to ask her about the cock pit.

"We filled it in, dear," she said. "It was disgusting."

CLOCKWISE, FROM LEFT: *The initial grind – I am sanding the front door with an orbital sander. An early morning shot of the Castle and garden with Otago Harbour in the background. The pointed fumerole behind the Castle is Harbour Cone. Me under the Cupola, about 1967.*

When Mr and Mrs Purdie installed electricity in the Castle in 1927, they bought a state of the art, split-level Moffat oven and cook-top. In 1967, 40 years on, this was my inheritance. No longer new, with a thermostat that didn't work, the split-level Moffat was my accomplice in the kitchen. I served teas on the upstairs veranda, except during January which was then our one busy month for visitors, when teas were served in the ballroom. I cooked fluffy white scones in that old Moffat oven every day for YEARS.

We decided to set up catering in the ballroom. This endeavour was rather curiously financed. In 1972 a student was found in possession of Larnach's skull and was charged with improperly interfering with human remains. It had previously been stolen from the Larnach family crypt in Dunedin's Northern Cemetery. A photograph of the skull with the bullet hole in the centre of the forehead appeared in the national newspaper, *Truth*. After the case, the police delivered the skull to the Castle in a red and white striped hatbox, thinking perhaps that they were bringing Larnach home. Embarrassed by this acquisition, Barry returned the skull to the Larnach family mausoleum.

The news of these events created such a public furore that a tide of inquisitive paying visitors swept through our doors. For the first time since buying the Castle, we had money in the bank. There was an auction at Wains Hotel, a gracious Victorian establishment in town. We used our unexpected financial windfall to purchase 100 matching upholstered oak dining chairs for the ballroom. We bought ovens, large pots and pans, an electric Zip water heater and a very large teapot. We were in business.

I was the caterer in the early years, which in those days involved interviewing the client, doing the costings and menus, buying and cooking the food and cleaning up after the function. I had helpers – my girls – one of whom, Heather Morris, is still employed at the Castle 30 years later. Yes, I was busy, producing all that food. I got thin and rather frantic. There was considerable human interest with weddings and celebrations but I wanted to be a gardener, not a cook.

Coiled within me was my plantsman's urge. Excitedly I explored the miracle of creating new plant life by sowing seeds, taking cuttings and making divisions. The progeny burgeoned all over the place and I set up a little shop to sell plants in the vinery. For 25 years, I produced rare and different plant stock that was seldom seen elsewhere. It was a wonderful way to gain an in-depth knowledge of plants.

For years it seemed that the grounds of the Castle took charge of us, not the other way around. In 1975 the pine plantations of Canterbury were felled by a great wind which also skirted coastal Otago. We spent a night of terror in the Castle listening to the roar of the storm. We awoke to a strange stillness, and looked in shock at the sight of the destruction which had radically altered the landscape. We were ringed by fallen trees, both young trees and century-old giants. Tree after tree had fallen between the Castle and the gate so that 26 trees lay across the drive. Power lines had been brought down, and fences crushed. Trees were lying bottoms up and tangled in their root balls were the severed sections of our precious water pipeline.

We had no water, no power, no phone, no fences, no road and no income. Our big chainsaw had been lent to a neighbour two kilometres away on the other side of the fallen trees. There was a danger to our children with the unstable trees and the fallen power cables, which were still partly live.

I can't remember how long it took us to gather ourselves together, and adjust to the situation. We had to get out of the Castle property to bring back our chainsaw and collect some milk. We needed to talk through the frightening experience with other people. Barry and I and the children climbed over and through the fallen trees on the drive. Outside our gate further colossal trees blocked the cutting in Camp Road. We reached the village of Pukehiki, where we retrieved the chainsaw and neighbours gave us some milk. We then went back to the Castle, again climbing through the fallen trees. At each

CLOCKWISE FROM OPPOSITE, TOP: *In my kitchen with the old Moffat oven on which I used to bake thousands of scones. The Castle at night broods on its nefarious past. Looking towards the gardener's cottage in the 1960s.*

ABOVE: *The entrance lions gaze across the garden.*
OPPOSITE, CLOCKWISE FROM TOP: *Norcombe peeps round from behind the 'Knave of Hearts' figure. Sophie poses for a picture in the rock garden, while I am more reluctant. Trevor Hall, now CEO of Tourism Holdings Ltd, begins his career in tourism by mowing the lawns at Larnach Castle. Norcombe joins him for the ride. I am barbecuing food for a children's birthday party.*

large branch or fallen trunk, Barry or I would go first, the children were helped through, the milk and chainsaw handed over and the other would then follow.

With the big chainsaw, our smaller chainsaw and the help of our farming neighbours, Jim and Sam Morris, a start was made in clearing a passageway through the drive. Dunedin City Council workers cleared the cutting on Camp Road. They cut a section out of each fallen tree trunk, wide enough for a car to drive through, then the sections were lifted by a crane onto the tray of a truck. The rings were counted on a giant macrocarpa and it was estimated that it had been planted in 1871, the year when the Castle building had begun. It took two years of our physical and financial resources to clear up and make good after this storm. Because it was an 'act of God', the only insurance that we could claim was $20 for a vase that had broken in the foyer.

Once they were big enough, the children helped with our multifarious tasks. Sophie's earliest memories are of running around the Castle with buckets to catch the leaks every time it rained. She and Norcombe sold ice creams in summer, picked up litter and joined in our projects. I was happy that they played in the garden, made huts and roamed the hillsides enjoying the same freedom that I had had as a child. They befriended the Wilmans, who farmed the land below the Castle, learning from them the lore of the countryside.

They ran away one day with some other children whose mothers were working at the Castle, and roamed overland south beyond Peggy's Hill, the highest point of the Peninsula. A light aircraft was flying low and they thought that their frantically worried parents back at the Castle had mounted a search. So they returned only to find that nobody had noticed they were missing.

The Castle roof was their playground, too. When Norcombe was just a little fellow, he gleefully found a short cut out of the second-floor bathroom window and across the roof to his bedroom. Sophie was the instigator when at night they crept out onto the veranda roof to watch the elaborately dressed guests arriving at our costumed balls. Two girls on a working holiday were staying with us and when I was away Norcombe stole their pantyhose and tied them to the Castle's Tudor chimneys.

A playground, a home, a vocation, the Castle was all of these things to our family, though it soaked up our time and energy like a gigantic greedy sponge. Meanwhile, outside the Castle doors, the garden lay waiting.

CHAPTER THREE

The Lost Rock Garden

One day, soon after we moved in, a Mr Ira Thornicroft came to visit. He lived in Tasmania, where he had been superintendent of the Hobart Botanical Gardens until he retired. He told us that he had laid out all of the gardens at Larnach Castle during the early 1930s for Mr J. Jackson Purdie.

"Where is the rock garden?" he asked.

"What rock garden?" we replied, as this was before we had discovered the glass negatives of the Purdie's time at the Castle and we had no idea that it had once been a centrepiece of the garden.

"But it was the biggest rock garden in New Zealand," he said, and he took us out to show us where it had been. A jungle of sycamore trees, self-sown macrocarpas, prickly berberis and blackberry had engulfed and obliterated the rock garden, which he had regarded as the most important part of his many developments here.

"My work has disappeared," he said, devastated to find no remnant of the bridge, pond, grotto and stream that had featured in the rockery which had spread over a third of a hectare.

LEFT: *The rock garden showing* Chiastophyllum oppositifolium *with yellow pendant racemes,* Blandfordia punicea, *and tall white-flowered* Asphodelus albus *in the background.* ABOVE: *The rock garden as it was in the 1930s when it was laid out by Ira Thornicroft.*

snow-covered mountains. I joined the newly formed Otago Alpine Garden Group and gained knowledge from more experienced members. I also joined the Scottish Rock Garden Club for its bulletins and annual seed exchange.

In 1976 I went to the First Interim International Rock Garden Conference in Seattle and Vancouver on the west coast of North America. At this event I went to lectures given by some of the outstanding people of the alpine plant world. The conference included a trip up Mount Ranier where for the first time I saw coloured flowers in the mountains. To my eyes, they looked like jewels. I read voraciously about alpine plants and how to grow them, about the special soil mixes and different growing aspects, about peat-loving plants and how to construct a scree garden. Then out I went to put this new knowledge into practice.

Each year I imported seeds through the seed exchange of the Scottish Rock Garden Club. This was before the bio-security laws which now prevent the importation of seed of new plants into the country. There was the thrill of germination when 'dust' from a numbered packet from the other side of the world was sown and sent up new little leaves. These plants were pricked out and nurtured, then planted into the garden. More excitement came with the first flower on a plant grown from seed; a flower that before I had only seen as a photograph in a book. I swapped seeds and plants with other enthusiasts and then there was always the sales table at the Otago Alpine Garden Group. I had plants, plants and more plants.

But some plants were such prima donnas that they refused to perform. Others were thugs and grew relentlessly, obliterating their neighbours. There were plants that were out of context or just frankly dingy. There were too many plants. I realised that I didn't have a garden, I had a stamp collection. A radical makeover was required.

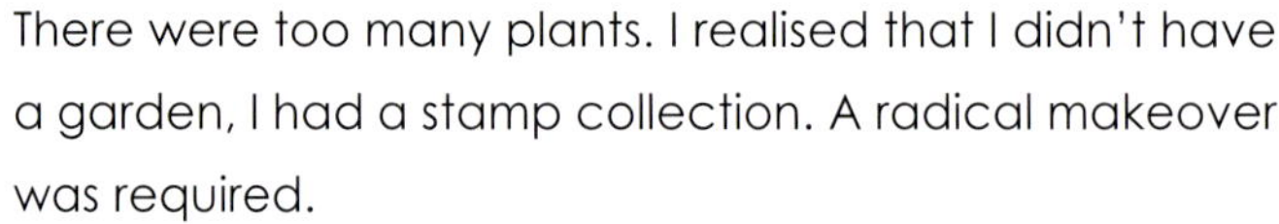

The plants were lifted and edited, and a lot went to the compost heap. Those that were replanted were sorted into themes by colour, taking into account the edaphic factor – that is, the soil conditions in which the plants grow in nature. I included a section for New Zealand's high altitude alpines. A scree slope was constructed for plants requiring superior drainage and a peat-enriched garden was made for dwarf rhododendrons and plants from the subantarctic islands.

Ranges of colours that complement or accentuate each other are grouped together and then separated by foliage from competing schemes. Red overwhelms delicate pastels, but given its own space makes a dramatic statement. A seasonal succession of red flowers, starting with *Anemone pavonina* and the creeping *Rhododendron* 'Carmen', continue until the kaffir

LEFT: *The Mount Cook lily* (Ranunculus lyallii). ABOVE: Phormium *'Red Fountain' with* Viola *'All Black' and* Anemone pavonina *(foreground), green* Euphorbia polychroma *and pink and red dwarf rhododendrons.*

lily of early winter, all supported by black mondo grass, dark-leafed euphorbia and, best of all, plant breeder Mark Jury's *Cordyline* 'Red Fountain'. Touches of sharp yellow from flowers including *Adonis amurensis* and the lime greens of *Hacquetia epipactis* and *Galtonia viridiflora* accentuate the scarlet.

This same scheme of supporting dark colours flows into the next area, highlighting flamboyant orange flowers and their blue companions. Early crown imperials, which are also called teardrop lilies, are enhanced by the blue drumstick primula (*Primula denticulata)* and the green-flowered *Helleborus foetidus*. Later, the aristocratic Christmas bells from Tasmania *(Blandfordia punicea)* bloom with the delicately veined northwest Pacific Coast irises.

A changing tapestry of flowers here includes the double Welsh orange poppy, cream and yellow primroses, blue violets, orange pansies and the perfumed yellow boronia. There are a few, but not too big, cream, apricot, blue and purple rhododendrons, which I hope are refined

LEFT: Fritillaria imperialis.
ABOVE: Blandfordia punicea.
OPPOSITE: Galtonia viridiflora *and* Cordyline *'Red Fountain'.*

and tasteful. Dark foliage to offset the luminosity of these flowers includes *Phormium* 'Platts Black', its thrusting spiky foliage contrasting with the rounded leaves of *Ligularia* 'Britt-Marie Crawford' and the dark, lacy, fern-like *Anthriscus* 'Raven's Wing'. Self-sown Bowles golden grass (*Milium effusum* 'Aureum') creates a shimmering haze through summer. Grey and silver foliage flows through and unifies other cooler colour groups. Pink and grey look pleasing together, as do yellow, blue and silver. Among the background shrubs are the silver-leafed New Zealand native olearias and brachyglottis. Aristocrats of the silver garden include New Zealand's own alpines, our raoulia, edelweiss and celmisias. They are clustered together in a high part of the rockery, their distinguished foliage more than compensating for the lack of flower colour. *Celmisia spedenii*, in particular, has foliage of spun aluminium.

Of their own accord, the crisp white *Trillium ovatum* have gone to bed amongst the silver *Astelia nivicola*. Who wouldn't want trilliums seeding in their garden? They look at home together so I have decided to leave them be.

An installation of cut and uncut stone placed in the lower rock garden was donated in 1998 by the residents of Broad Bay to commemorate their historical connection to the Castle. The work that Larnach had given the early settlers had helped to found their community, as stone and all other materials for building the Castle had been hauled straight up the steep 300-metre hill from Broad Bay, nestled by the harbour below.

Over 100 years later descendants of the labourers and builders of the Castle and other members of the Broad Bay community again walked up the hill wearing Victorian costume. On this beautiful summer's day they got extremely hot on the strenuous climb because of the weight of their period outfits; the women in particular felt sorry for their ancestors having to wear such voluminous clothing every day. They were accompanied by a horse-drawn sled carrying blocks of cut stone, symbolising the work of the stone masons who built the castle.

The stone was donated by the Dunedin City Council and the then Mayor of Dunedin, Sukhi Turner, rode the sled for part of the way. It was not very comfortable so the local policeman, Lox Kellas, brought her across country in his four-wheel drive police car for the remainder of the journey. About 70 of us joined together in the installation ceremony performed by the Mayor and, after she had planted a tree, we all had afternoon tea.

TOP: *A nomocharis hybrid with* Diplarrhena moraea, *an Australian plant of the iris family.*
ABOVE: *Broad Bay residents walking up the hill wearing Victorian costume during celebrations of their historic connection with the Castle.*
OPPOSITE, TOP: Celmisia semicordata. OPPOSITE: *The scree garden.*

This was the Broad Bay community's way of celebrating the 150th anniversary of the founding of the City of Dunedin.

In the future I intend to take out some more mixed planting and to mass plant instead some singular New Zealand native plants, including celmisias, the iconic Mount Cook lily, not a lily but *Ranunculus lyallii,* and the magnificent megaherb *Stilbocarpa polaris,* from the subantarctic islands. I am growing the *Stilbocarpa* from seed. The aim is to simplify the planting and to provide an interesting sequence for the visitor from one scheme to the next. To create the appropriate ambience, the centre of the rock garden is high and open to the sky, as are the mountains where alpine plants originate, and it is paved with rectangular concrete pavers to counterpoint the natural rocks.

Clive and Nicki Higgie – creators of Paloma, the stunningly original garden near Wanganui – call this design element the 'helicopter landing pad'. In contrast to the open space, a meandering back path is left overgrown. Slightly dark and mysterious, it is a reminder of the past – my past as a child in another garden and the Castle garden of the past.

The other day I heard children talking on this path: "Isn't this exciting?" they whispered to one another. "I hope we don't get lost."

ABOVE: *A secret back path in the rock garden.*
OPPOSITE, TOP: *The rock garden showing the 'helicopter landing pad' at the centre left.*
OPPOSITE: *Sophie as a child in the ruined garden.*

CHAPTER FOUR

The Serpentine Walk

I first planted a perennial border in the 1970s when little conifers were all the rage. Then pebble gardens became trendy – polythene sheets were laid on the ground, holes were cut through the plastic for the plants, and then the rest of the sheeting was covered in pebbles. But while all this was happening elsewhere, I planted more flowers.

My border survived the herb garden phase. Then suddenly mass-planted lavender became *à la mode*. Briefly my border was fashionable, even ahead of its time, when 'cottage gardening' was the prevailing taste. I resisted doing a makeover of the border into a potager, despite the publicity generated by the English garden writer Rosemary Verey's detailed example with its narrow paths at her home, Barnsley.

I stood aloof from the green tailored look with box, mondo grass and white flowers. I stuck with my colourful flowers through the following phase of minimalism and metal installations. Auckland went troppo, but I didn't try that in Dunedin. Now we are being told to revegetate with eco-sourced plant material. Flower borders are now thought of as frivolous and watering them is viewed as an irresponsible waste of the world's limited resources. Through all of these fashions, I remained faithful to my old love, a style from long ago born of leisured days in Edwardian summer gardens.

A path manages a visitor's journey through a garden. I put in a serpentine path in the Castle's garden to slow down people and to allow the flower beds to be displayed to them from a full frontal view,

I groom the Serpentine Walk. The grass path has recently been replaced with a new landscaped path.

CHAPTER FIVE

A Step Out from the Ballroom

Larnach built it for his girls. He began a new wing for the Castle with a 27-metre ballroom in 1886. He hoped that his daughters would stay at home but when Alice and Colleen returned to the Castle after eight years in Europe, they got bored and took off for Christchurch. Kate, the eldest, died of typhoid when just a young woman in her twenties. It is said her body was laid in the ballroom in a glass coffin with a rose on her breast. The then redundant ballroom was only used for drying the washing.

After Larnach's death and the subsequent sale of the Castle to the government, the ballroom became a ward of the mental hospital. An elderly medical practitioner, who had returned to Dunedin in 1969 for the centenary of Otago University, visited the Castle and told me that he had worked here during World War I.

"So many New Zealand doctors were at the front in Europe that medical students were called upon to do their work back home," he told me.

"Was it a hospital then?" I asked.

"It was a lunatic asylum," he replied. "And all the patients had

LEFT: *The ballroom being used as a film set for Hanlon, a television programme about a nineteenth century Dunedin lawyer. Members of the Otago District Law Society played extras for a turn-of-the-century ball.*
ABOVE: *The Castle before the ballroom was built, showing the planting of macrocarpa trees on what is now the ballroom lawn.*

chilblains and diarrhoea. The Castle hasn't changed much," he added. *Oh dear*.

Mrs Purdie had used the ballroom as a display and salesroom for antiques during the 1930s and also served teas. When the Castle was leased in 1939 it became a nightclub, then sheep were kept in the ballroom during the forties and fifties. People still remember it being used as a holding pen. Ralph Maxwell, a local carrier, used to load the sheep and truck them to the freezing works.

Nowadays the ballroom is a café where our visitors can take coffee, teas and lunch in elegant surroundings. In winter, we keep all three of the great log fires burning. As evening comes, there are weddings, balls, dinners and celebrations under the glittering chandeliers. We hold the Winter Ball every year in June. For a few magical hours the Castle returns to the Victorian era, with gentlemen in tailcoats and ladies in period gowns dancing the Sir Roger de Coverley and the Dashing White Sergeant.

Other diverse scenes have played out: a memorial service for a friend's son who had died climbing in the Himalayas; washing machines have been launched for Fisher and Paykel, and many film makers have used the ballroom as a set. There have been orchestral concerts and fashion parades and, most memorably, a play.

Michealanne Forster was commissioned to write *Larnach Castle of Lies* for the Court theatre in Christchurch. It was a sensational drama of the Larnach family's life – the quarrelling daughters, the betrayal of Larnach by his third wife and son, Larnach's suicide. The play was staged in Dunedin by the Fortune Theatre Company in 1994. To make a memorable first night, the theatre company decided to hold a once-only performance of the play at the protagonist's home, Larnach Castle, in the ballroom built by him with such hope.

On the afternoon before this special night, the company held a rehearsal in the ballroom. All went well. A hundred important people, newspaper reporters and potential sponsors for the theatre company, were invited to what promised to be a memorable evening. It was a lovely night, calm at first. Guests arrived and were seated in the ballroom where fires had been lit in the three fireplaces. The play began. Suddenly a storm came up. The smoke blew back down the chimneys and into the room so that the audience couldn't see. We opened the tops of the windows to let out some of the smoke. The fury of the wind blew the curtains sideways across the room which turned clammily cold.

The heavens opened and a rainstorm pelted down onto the iron roof so noisily that we could not hear the actors speak. Some malevolent outside force was at work. It was turning this re-enactment in Larnach's home of his tragic last years into a fiasco. The actor playing Larnach went onto the stage for his last act of the drama, the taking of his own life. He put the gun to his head and pulled the trigger. There was a flash of red, then the ballroom was lit by a blinding white light.

During supper after the play, everybody was talking.

"How sinister – lightning flashed just as Larnach shot himself," many in the audience commented.

"Oh no," I said. "That was a staged lighting effect. Let's ask the producer."

He confirmed that the flash of white light was not his doing. Some meddling outside phenomenon had made mischief in the night. Was Larnach not wanting his final tragedy laid bare for an inquisitive audience?

Larnach had planted pine trees for shelter in front of and behind the ballroom. In time these grew until they met overhead, so that when Mr J. Jackson Purdie bought the Castle in 1927, the ballroom was lost in the woods.

The Purdies clear-felled the area in front of the ballroom up to the drive and laid out a lawn, with patterned beds in the Victorian style, probably designed by Mr Ira Thornicroft. There were two sickle-shaped beds and a Maltese Cross for the bedding out of annuals enclosed by a semi-circular perennial border with a few shrubs dotted in. This design was obliterated over the years except for the shrubs which had assumed voluminous proportions. A buddleja was quite 12 metres through. Aged rhododendrons with yellow leaves, indicating bad drainage, were reverting to thickets of ponticum rootstock.

We identified issues with the ballroom and its setting. The entry to the ballroom was from the driveway through doors in an 18-metre passage which connected it to the Castle. The ballroom itself, with no doors to the garden, presented a blank face and was unconnected to the surrounding grounds. Perhaps it was built that way because they had the wind to contend with then, and life was lived differently. Now, long grass grew against the front wall and a badly laid concrete path put down in the forties was breaking up. The splendid architecture was masked by the old shrubs, which looked like lumps on the lawn.

There were logistics to consider. Delivery vehicles were required to drive right down the front of the ballroom to the kitchen door. In front of and adjacent to the ballroom was a sheltered area with the potential for people to sit out, and for receptions. This space required suitable access from different directions by foot. Planting needed to enhance, not disguise, the building and to reflect its symmetry. The spatial design was to be viewed from the tower above, as well as from the drive and all around the front, and needed to key into the site.

But I wanted the garden to sing, to fulsomely flower and tell of the passing seasons, to flow and ripple across the lawn. I drew flowing lines on paper. There was a half circle in front of the ballroom for a forecourt and reception area with fluid,

CLOCKWISE FROM LEFT: *The lawn in front of the ballroom shortly after we arrived. The Rock Garden was beneath the growth seen at the top of the photograph. The ballroom, taken from the tower in about 1935, showing the Patterned Garden and planting. My drawings for the Patterned Garden.*

enclosing beds to be filled with flowering plants. The design was symmetrical, with paths at each end and leading through the middle, and centred on the ballroom. The beds were to be surrounded by the existing lawn which connected the front drive to the Rock Garden.

We tackled this task in 1981: first there was the destruction, then the excavation. The lumps on the lawn got the chop. Only the two tall anchoring fastigiate yews were retained. The broken concrete path was taken away and the half-circle forecourt area excavated to a depth of 45 centimetres. A drain was laid and gravel brought in. Barry prided himself in having calculated $\pi r^{2's}$ correctly so that we knew we needed exactly nine truck loads of gravel. This was raked and rolled and we had our new forecourt, and the delivery drive to the kitchen door.

A student that summer installed the double brick edging of the gravelled area. The next step was to transfer my flowing designs for the surrounding planting beds from paper to the ground. I sat, with the drawings in hand, on the ballroom roof while I called to Barry, who laid and adjusted ropes on the existing lawn. With the current health and safety laws I would not be allowed to sit there nowadays. Our foreman, John Murray, sprayed the lawn within the enclosing ropes with Roundup and plenty of magenta spray to dye-mark the area.

ABOVE: *The Patterned Garden in the mist showing pink and white ericas with* Gladiolus papilio *and purple* Thalictrum delavayi *'Hewitt's Double'*. OPPOSITE: *The Patterned Garden with the heathers in full bloom and the azaleas corralled by the box hedge.*

"Why is the grass that colour?" a visitor asked Barry, who told them that we had put in grass seed from Russia.

Planting beds were dug and raised using our own compost, coke breeze and pine needles from under the trees. Deciduous azaleas were planted around the forecourt, enclosed by beds of heathers and ericas. The azaleas were bought from Denis Hughes of Blue Mountain Nurseries at Tapanui, who supplied 'Ilam' varieties and some of his own breeding. Box hedging was threaded through to mask the azalea legs and add structure. Totara topiaries act as sentinels on the centre path and the fastigiate yews from the 1930s, surrounded by clipped hebes, anchored the edges of the design.

This garden proclaims seasonal change. I am so glad we have winter because then there is spring. In July, beneath the naked wood of the azaleas, ink-blue *Iris histrioides* 'Major' brave the worst of the weather. They are followed in August by dainty crocus *(Crocus chrysanthus)* varieties, which only open their inwardly lit chalices when the sun shines, conserving their beauty. September brings miniature

---

ABOVE: *Snow on the azaleas and totara topiaries. Totara is naturally a New Zealand forest tree.*
OPPOSITE: *Spring and the azaleas in bloom.*

narcissi and the crown imperial *(Fritillaria imperialis)* with stems of elegant black encircled by a cluster of orange nodding bells which are topped by a leafy green crown. Its other epithet, tear drop lily, describes the five teardrops suspended within each bell. Legend has it that this proud lily, then milky white, refused to bow its head to Jesus as He entered the Garden of Gethsemane. Then, overcome with shame, it blushed and bent its head of tears for ever after.

Soon, the tissue-paper-textured azaleas burst into bloom in clear bright colours in the sharp spring light. Orange, scarlet, apricot and pink are blended with cream. Clipped balls of totara topiary sit above the shimmering sheen of colour. This sumptuous display is backed by the warm gold and ochre of the sandstone ballroom and the dark green yews, and is encompassed by the textured heather and spring-green lawn.

After the longest day, dainty, dwarf pink and white cyclamen *(Cyclamen hederifolium)* remind us that the seasons move on. Heathers and ericas take front stage in swirls of pink, purple and white. Lavender-coloured *Colchicum speciosum*, like giant crocuses, bigger, coarser, more showy but not related at all, provide colour under the azaleas. Above float clouds of dainty purple *Thalictrum delavayi* 'Hewitts Double', like dark-stained gypsophila.

Time moves on. The flowers fade. Azalea leaves turn burgundy, and spent blooms in the heathers take on the muted old rose and russet colours of an ancient tapestry. Bright green ribbons of box contrast sharply. Sometimes in winter, snow settles on the fretted framework of the bare branches of the azaleas, outlining the box ribbons and capping the topiaries. Again we await the spring.

The ballroom garden is out front and always on parade, and is most carefully managed by our head gardener, Fiona Eadie. As the azaleas grew, plants were taken out and others reshuffled to blend the colours. They are pruned and thinned annually immediately after flowering to keep the height within the design and the balance between the spring and autumn displays. We enjoy the tawny seed heads of the heathers so they are clipped back just before new growth in spring. If they are not clipped back, plants grow tired and woody.

Even so, after about fifteen years, the heathers and ericas were started again from tip cuttings and the old plants removed and replaced. The box hedge is clipped twice in the season, in mid-spring and again in the autumn in time for the hedge to recover before winter. Hebes are clipped, fed and limed. Crown imperials are given a fertiliser high in potash to build up the bulbs. In late summer azaleas are given that same fertiliser to ripen the wood in our soft climate and to encourage the formation of flower buds.

The fastigiate yews had grown pot bellied with age and splayed out in heavy snow. They were cut back to a few tall sticks which were roped in and tied. A post hole digger was used to make holes in the root zone which were filled with a nitrogenous fertiliser to kick-start the old wood into new growth.

Some American friends had taken me to Filoli, near San Francisco, to see the columnar yews (as seen on the television soap *Dynasty*) being cut back. I photographed the process and brought the knowledge home. The treatment was successful. Many people with old gardens populated by yews with middle-aged spread called up the same arborist, Ewan Cadzow, to do a 'Margaret Barker', as liposuction on yews in Dunedin came to be called.

Our carefully constructed forecourt, now enclosed by elegant flowering surroundings, was constantly in use on fine evenings for pre-dinner drinks. But the problem remained of complicated access to the ballroom, which turned a blind eye to the garden. The ballroom's 27-metre-long wall was punctuated by six arches, each with a set of three deeply recessed, narrow windows. In 2005 we decided to take out the two central sets of windows and their stone surrounds and to install glass-panelled doors within the existing arches.

THIS PAGE, TOP: *Norcombe puts some weight on the roller as the forecourt is gravelled. The set of windows on the left have been removed and replaced with glass-panelled doors.*
ABOVE: *The new doors which connect the ballroom to the outdoor café and Patterned Garden.*
OPPOSITE: *Sophie entertains friends in our delightful open-air café.*

We consulted the architectural firm of Mason and Wales who had designed the ballroom wing for Larnach and who still had the original plans. The entrance doors to the Castle were measured and studied for proportions, design, construction and the use of wood. Plans were drawn for new doors, which were approved by the Historic Places Trust and the Dunedin City Council. Gary Turner of Stevenson and Williams made the new doors from Tasmanian oak. This is the marketing name for the similar timbers of *Eucalyptus regnans* and *E. delagatensis*, identified as the same wood used for the entrance doors to the Castle. Bronze door handles and finger plates were cast from those on the Castle doors.

Thank goodness I was in far away Perth in Western Australia the day the dreadful deed was done by the stone-cutter making holes in the 120-year-old ballroom wall. The stonework was refinished and a new keystone, cut from the surplus sandstone, was put in by Castle employee Nathan Kelly. The new doors were installed by Paul Fahey.

Times and usages change and move on, as do the seasons, and the Castle evolves to meet them. The ballroom now connects with the forecourt and faces out to the garden, with its ballet of seasonal change, and to the visitors who have come to enjoy. On warm evenings, guests at parties can drift from the ballroom out to the garden. From this coming spring, our café will spill into the forecourt. Visitors can sit on delicate chairs among the azaleas and drink New Zealand wine. The doors open up a refreshing new era.

CHAPTER SIX

Slowly, Slowly I Find My Way

It is said that you learn from your mistakes. My only regret is that it took me so long to find my way. Like many young gardeners, I was caught in the grip of Sissinghurst. The garden created by Vita Sackville-West and Harold Nicolson at the once derelict Sissinghurst Castle in the English County Kent continues to be inspirational to generations of gardeners around the world. I, too, read Vita Sackville-West's collected columns from the *Observer* newspaper; and Vita and Harold's letters and books telling of the creation of the garden at Sissinghurst.

Sissinghurst has many aspects. The one that I particularly aspired to emulate was the romantic display of 'old' roses. At that stage, I had never visited this feted garden on the other side of the world. Even so, in my imagination I saw roses clambering up and festooning the walls of Larnach Castle.

I learnt all I could about old and shrub roses. I studied books and came to know gallicas, damasks, mosses and bourbons and their interesting histories. I visited New Zealand's famed rose expert Nancy Steen and was privileged to be shown around her enchanting garden in Auckland. I bought many old rose plants from the Masons of Palmerston North and planted them all about the garden. The plants grew all right, but the leaves went mouldy and they hardly ever flowered. The few blooms that struggled to appear rotted and went brown. I persevered for a number of years, but eventually my romantic notions were dashed on the altar of reality. Roses would not thrive in

A copper beech with New Zealand's iconic cabbage tree (Cordyline australis).

our soft, moist, maritime climate. Larnach Castle was not to be wreathed in their blooms.

Diane and Peter Arthur came to stay. This was before they founded their famous mail order company Touchwood Books, which now sells gardening books around the world. But both of them were already keen gardeners, and Diane was particularly interested in 'old' roses.

"If you dig them up," I said to Peter, "Diane can have my whole collection." One plant, 'Souvenir de la Malmaison', was growing high into a totara tree. Peter cut it down with a chainsaw. They took it back with the others to Waikonini Station, their home in Hawke's Bay, where it was dropped in a hole. It thrives there to this day.

But I kept my 'Mermaid' rose. It fights back when pruned in winter, flinging out its exuberant growth to grip the gardener who does the deed, lacerating her with its vicious thorns. The leaves develop mildew in our moist summers but all is forgiven if we have a dry spell with warm winds from the northwest. Then the perfumed moonlight flowers, with a central dark boss of stamens, float from the gold-and-amber-veined sandstone of the ballroom wall.

It was after I had come to terms with my failure to grow roses that I first visited Sissinghurst. I was staying with a friend in London and we waited until the roses came out before making our journey down to Kent. From Victoria Station we took a train to Tunbridge Wells. We then caught the local bus to the village of Sissinghurst. We walked the rest of the way for about an hour, through the fields in the summer sunshine, buying fragrant strawberries at a roadside stall. I was enraptured by the romance of the garden at Sissinghurst Castle. Shrub roses were encouraged to cascade and flow. Lush underplantings of paeonies, geraniums, penstemons, alliums and salvias were in sympathetic colours. We climbed the tower to view the garden in its setting of the surrounding Kent countryside, and the perfume of the roses floated up to us on the still air. This visit confirmed my conclusion that our dark windswept volcanic peninsula where giant albatrosses fly is not a bit like the fields of Kent. I had to garden for our own, different land.

Mists swirl around Larnach Castle. Dark conifers comb the water-bearing winds blowing from off the sea, capturing the moisture which drips from the trees. In the early days of our tenure, these gloomy giants were too close to the house, casting their dark shade. When the light was low in autumn, I longed for bright flames of colour. I imagined luminous torches of deciduous trees, brilliant against the velvet green background of macrocarpa and pines.

I set about the task of creating this scene with alacrity. With considerable difficulty and over a period of time, the large macrocarpas, pines and Lawson's cypresses that were too close to the house were removed; and their ominous presences were not mourned. I read about deciduous trees in the books from England which were the only ones available then. I planted many different deciduous trees, one of each, which I had read about in these books. I also planted forms that had yellow or purple foliage.

Now I am pleased that most of these coloured cultivars died. The trees grew in spring as expected, and they continued to grow in summer when the wood should have ripened. In our soft moist climate

---

OPPOSITE: *Roses failed but as a compensation the legendary blue poppies* (Meconopsis betonicifolia) *thrive. Here they are shown with the Stable and copper beech tree in the background. The Stable is now used as accommodation for guests.* ABOVE: *Autumn-coloured foliage of European beech frames the Castle.*

growth continued through autumn. In winter, the leaves went brown and mushy and the soft unripened wood was frosted back. These were supposed to be hardy trees! I could not understand what was happening.

I planted nearly 30 ornamental cherry trees which would flower in spring in addition to having autumn colour. I did what I thought were clever things. Two double white *Prunus serrulata* 'Mt Fuji' were positioned to eventually hold hands and create a beautiful bower for brides. Three fastigiate *Prunus* 'Amanogawa' were grouped with a weeping pink rosebud cherry. Their leaves were attacked by fungus disease, the trunks leaked gum and branches died back. Those few trees that did not die of their own accord were helped out with the chainsaw. I learnt that I could not succeed with woody plants from continental climates with definite seasons – hot summers to ripen the wood and cold winters to give the plants a rest. This bitter journey of trying to establish deciduous trees just as I had seen them growing in English books took up ten years of my gardening life.

Fleur Snedden, the great-great granddaughter of Larnach, had researched his work and life. She told me that Larnach had planted many deciduous trees. Where were they now? Had he trod the same path, and experienced the same failures? But his successful trees were all around us in majestic maturity. What trees would succeed on my peninsula site?

The evidence had been before me all the time in the monumental macrocarpa trees, the reptilian monkey puzzle from the snow-capped Andes of South America, a glossy northern rata from our own coasts, and layered cedar trees from the Atlas Mountains and the Indian Himalayas. Aged and twisted rhododendrons spoke of misted mountains in China. There was some autumn colour from the European beech *(Fagus sylvatica)*. In the Alps of France I had walked amongst glades of such beeches growing in meadows of blue cranesbill geraniums, fluffy pink *Thalictrum aquilegifolium* and stately *Gentian lutea*. All of these trees had thrived in our grounds for many decades. All came from maritime or montane sites, from mild moist climates similar to that of the Otago Peninsula. It was to these places that I must look for trees and plants for my own garden.

I had seen photographs of southern Chile, which has a moist climate just as experienced here. Monkey puzzles grew there with other

ABOVE: *A cherry tree struggles amongst the long grass. It eventually succumbed to fungal diseases.* RIGHT: *The Barker family with descendants of William Larnach, from left to right, Jim Snedden, Bianco, Norcombe Barker, Margaret Barker, Sophie Barker, Fleur Snedden with her grandchildren Fleur and Nicholas Allen.* OPPOSITE: *An aerial view from the north of the Castle and grounds. The Lodge accommodation is in the foreground with the South Seas Garden to right.*

trees that coloured the mountain sides red and gold in autumn. What trees were these? They were southern beeches – *Nothofagus alpina (*syn *N. procera)* and *N. antarctica* – deciduous trees which were closely related to New Zealand's evergreen beeches. I planted these Chilean forms and they have proved successful, turning soft autumn colours in May. I tried *N. obliqua* from drier central Chile. It continues to grow through to July and does not colour here, but it is a wonderful tree for Wanaka and inland Otago.

Doreen Borland, who had worked at the Castle for seventeen years, received much joy from the mature European beech at the car park entrance. On her retirement, she donated and planted a young beech nearby to mark her years at the Castle and to give pleasure to future visitors and staff. I have planted many more of these beeches over the years. They are a favourite tree, happy here, and create seasonal beauty. Their soft green spring growth weeps gracefully, the young trees poised and resembling dancers. In autumn the leaves turn from green to gold then russet. Starting from the top of the tree, the colours change downwards in layers, a different hue greeting you each day. I cannot attain the famed cacophony of colour of Central Otago in autumn but, nevertheless, the changing of the seasons at Larnach Castle is gently radiant.

Beeches are planted behind sharply clipped evergreen hedges, and the afternoon sun shines through their golden leaves, illuminating these trees against the background of dark sheltering conifers. When I was young I tried many different trees. Now I prefer the calming effect of many of the same tree, simplifying the scene.

We still plant macrocarpas *(Cupressus macrocarpa)*, not close to the house but as a first defence and background. These Californian trees are characteristic of New Zealand's modified landscape, sheltering farmlands and rural homesteads from Northland to Bluff. Local albatrosses might enjoy the regular gales but most people and plants do not, needing the shelter the macrocarpas can provide. Even at an altitude of 300 metres, we can get blasted with salt from the sea. I visited the Monterey Peninsula in America to see macrocarpas, locally called the Monterey cypress, growing wild in their own place right on the coast and saw that they had evolved in salt winds.

In San Francisco, I first saw the potential of macrocarpas that had been pruned by arborists. With a clean-out of dead and extraneous wood, they stood revealed as sculptural landmarks. In New Zealand, their battered untidiness is disregarded as utilitarian, like an old shed. I came home from San Francisco and called up an arborist. After limbing up and shaping, our aged macrocarpas now stand proud in the landscape.

The planting of roses and deciduous trees were the first faltering steps of a lifetime's journey of discovery and expression. Which plants would grow and thrive here? How could my garden convey the underlying truth of this site?

At first my search for suitable plants was conducted from reading books and catalogues and looking at other people's gardens, but the time came when I could go out into the field to see plants growing in natural places.

An early journey was to Tasmania, where I saw King Billy's pine (*Athrotaxis selaginoides)* and, gliding along by boat on the Gordon River, the famed Huon pine *(Lagarostrobos franklinii)*. This beautiful weeping conifer is a relative of our New Zealand rimu. A long-lived tree, it is renowned for its decorative timber, which tends not to rot. By matching the growth rings of living trees with trunks long fallen on the ground, scientists have been able to track the climate of Tasmania going back for 10,000 years. They have established that, in this period, the climate stayed much the same until the 1950s when it started to warm.

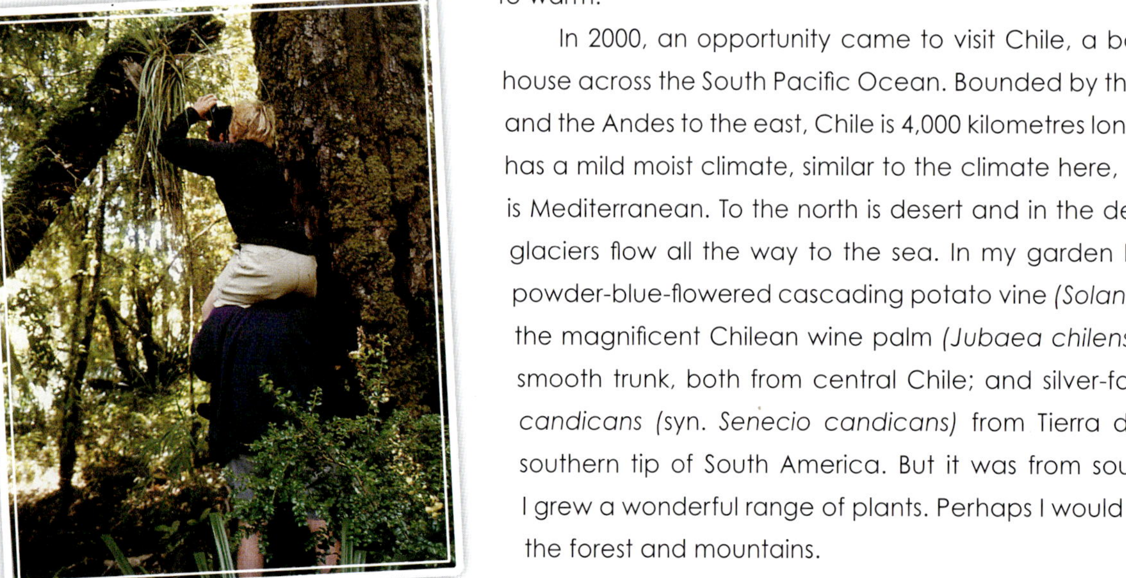

In 2000, an opportunity came to visit Chile, a botanical treasure house across the South Pacific Ocean. Bounded by the sea to the west and the Andes to the east, Chile is 4,000 kilometres long. Southern Chile has a mild moist climate, similar to the climate here, but central Chile is Mediterranean. To the north is desert and in the deep, deep south, glaciers flow all the way to the sea. In my garden I grew puya, the powder-blue-flowered cascading potato vine *(Solanum crispum)* and the magnificent Chilean wine palm *(Jubaea chilensis)*, with its wide, smooth trunk, both from central Chile; and silver-foliaged *Cineraria candicans* (syn. *Senecio candicans)* from Tierra del Fuego at the southern tip of South America. But it was from southern Chile that I grew a wonderful range of plants. Perhaps I would discover more in the forest and mountains.

Unlike New Zealand, a newly found land, Chile was settled by people who crossed the land bridge from Siberia to Alaska and who reached all of South America by the twelfth century BC. The Spanish conquistadors arrived in the sixteenth century and settled central Chile, but the Mapuche, or Araucarian, Indians, of central and southern Chile were not fully conquered until the late nineteenth century. Even so, much of the natural habitat has been modified, with tracts of forest cleared for farming.

I went to Chile with a small group led by botanist Dr Peter Wardle and his wife Margaret. On Christmas Eve, we travelled from Auckland to Buenos Aires, the capital of Argentina, then back west to Santiago in central Chile, crossing the Andes twice. We flew over southern Chile's snow-covered volcanic cones, mysterious in the evening light. These mountains have witnessed the earth's most violent forces.

Our first day in Chile was Christmas Day and Robyn Kilty, my travelling companion, and I went to a church on Santiago's Plaza de Armas. On Boxing Day we travelled east to the Andes to El Morado National Park at 1,900 metres where we camped. Camped! I hadn't camped since I was nine years old when my younger brother and I put up a pup tent on the family's front lawn.

Robyn and I struggled in the wind to slip the metal reinforcing rods into the slots of the slapping polypropylene tent. That done, we had to control the recalcitrant beast in the fierce wind by pegging it down. But how? The ground was all bumpy rock. We had plenty of pegs but no hammer to bang them in. On the next site, Mary and Andrew McEwen showed us how to hammer them in with a stone. Nothing wrong with Stone Age tools! We blew up our mattresses and stuffed some clothes into pillowslips for pillows, then wriggled into our sleeping bags to get some sleep. The mattresses were quite thin and you didn't have to be a princess to feel the rocks underneath.

With the altitude, the cold and the jet lag, I was suddenly awake at 2am requiring the *baños*. Where was my torch in this dark little tent? I couldn't find it – such bad organisation. I pulled out a few warm clothes from my pillowslip, put them on and fiddled around with the zips on the tent, which was firmly sealed up against tarantulas. I got out of the tent and saw the bridge that straddled the raging torrent of snow melt from the Andes. I crossed the bridge and continued under some trees to where I could see the white painted *baños* in the starlight.

Then the time came to walk back under the trees – and the starlight was blacked out. I couldn't see the bridge, or anything at all. I mustn't panic, I said to myself, or I might fall into the rushing waters of the snow melt and get washed down to the Pacific Ocean. I quietly felt my way around until later, much later, I eventually found the bridge. I crossed it and once out of the trees I could see my way back to our tent in the returning starlight.

OPPOSITE: *My photography reaches new heights with a lift from Rodney Lewington in a rainforest in southern Chile.* ABOVE: *We set up camp in Argentina.*

We awoke in the crisp, clear light of the Andes and trekked upwards through marvellous wildflowers towards a glacier. Helen Clark, New Zealand's Prime Minister at the time, was on the other side of the mountain attempting a climb from Argentina. After about two hours of walking gently upwards, we came upon the legendary wreath nasturtium *(Tropaeolum polyphyllum)*, tantalisingly rare in gardens and difficult to grow. Its steel-grey filigree foliage emerged from the melting snow and grew in flowing trails clustered with golden nasturtium flowers.

There were thousands of plants, sometimes making a colourful picture with purple and pink *Schizanthus hookerii*, which is commonly called poor man's orchid although, like many South American plants, including the potato, it is a solanum. I have only seen this tropaeolum three times in cultivation – at Sissinghurst in Kent, at Helen Dillon's in Dublin and at Rosamund Banks' garden in Herefordshire. Rosamund showed me how she grew the alpine nasturtium in a well-drained bed that was raised about a metre. I have recently acquired this treasure and have planted it raised and in gravel. I hope it survives as a memento of my Andean adventure.

We drove north from Santiago where the countryside becomes dryer and turns into puya and cactus country. We visited a cloud forest above the semi-desert slopes. The scant rainfall was supplemented by the moisture-bearing winds that came in off the Humboldt current, then turned into cloud as they rose and cooled. The dripping trees collected the moisture from the clouds which sustained a rainforest of ancient plants, like an island in the dry cordillera. Here were *Drimys winteri*, or winter's bark, which

ABOVE: Tropaeolum polyphyllum, *a nasturtium found high in the Chilean Andes, inland from Santiago.*
OPPOSITE: Asteranthera ovata *in a rainforest in southern Chile.*

we were to see again far to the south at Peurto Montt, and *Griselinia scandens*, uncannily similar to our New Zealand *Griselinia lucida*.

We turned back and drove south on the Pan-Americana highway, eventually reaching southern Chile. Here was a climate similar to that of Dunedin. In the central valley near Temuco, in a remnant of virgin forest, *Eucryphia cordifolia*, smothered in creamy white flowers, soared to 30 metres. In the shops at home it was sold as a shrub. I would call it a tree. There was *Luma apiculata* with its myrtle flowers and remarkable cinnamon bark, and *Lapageria rosea* or copihue, the Chilean national flower with deep, rose-coloured, pendulous waxen trumpets.

From Peurto Montt we travelled to Los Alerces Andinos National Park to see Patagonian cypresses *(Fitzroya cupressoides)* which Chilean scientists maintain are the longest lived trees in the world. These trees grow in a very wet climate, but the more accessible ones have been harvested for their timber. To see the large *Fitzroya* and return was an eight-hour tramp through mud. It was a spectacular and varied rainforest with a vast array of evergreen plants and trees and many beautiful flowers. There were fuchsias and gunneras, the little *G. magellanica* and that giant brute *G. tinctoria*; guevina, azara and pernettya with berries of many colours; desfontainea with orange and yellow flowers like dead goldfish, and escalonias. The tricuspidaria had waxen, strawberry-coloured lanterns. *Mitraria coccinea* scrambled up other shrubs, decorating them with its tubular scarlet flowers. We resolutely tramped on in the mud, past the many diversions, until we came upon the vast trunks of the venerable *Fitzroya*. These ruggedly aged trees were growing here before the birth of Christ yet they were delicately wreathed in the pretty pink hanging trumpet flowers of *Philesia magellanica*, a scandent lapageria relative.

At an impromptu stop by the side of the road we saw the luminous ruby flowers of *Asteranthera ovata*, caught in a flicker of sunlight. Peter Wardle described my expression as rapture at the discovery of this rare jewel that I had never seen before. It is a delicate climber that thrives only where it is mild, partly shady and the air, as well as the ground, is moist.

I had thought on leaving Chile that I would not see this treasure again, but then Gordon Collier mentioned that 'we' brought it back from Brodick, a Gulf Stream garden on the west coast of Scotland, when you were allowed to do such things. There was a plant at Pukeiti, a magnificent garden of rhododendrons and other exotics planted in the native forest on the slopes of Mt Taranaki. Graham Smith, the garden's director, kindly couriered me a cutting of *Asteranthera*, which is now established in the fog garden behind the ballroom. It is a reminder of that moment of joy in a forest in southern Chile, and of friendships shared among gardeners.

As time moved on I became inspired more by what I saw growing in natural wild places than by what I read about in books.

CHAPTER SEVEN

A New Vision

Dunedin is often called the 'Edinburgh of the South'. The traditions of the Scottish settlers linger, particularly the importance placed on education. Dunedin has New Zealand's first university and, like Edinburgh, a famous medical school. The Scottish poet Robbie Burns is celebrated with a sculpture in the centre of the city. Scottish gardeners going from the old land to the new brought with them skills and knowledge so that now in Dunedin there are many beautifully tended public and private gardens.

These gardens feature woodland plantings with rhododendrons and alpine and rock gardens. Many of the plants grown are those which were first brought back to Scotland from the Himalayas by their great botanical explorers Forrest, Sheriff and, more recently, the Cox family. This type of gardening is very successful in Dunedin, even though our climate is considerably warmer than that of Scotland.

Dunedin gardening mentors suggested that I go to Scotland, the 'mother country', to study the acme of this type of gardening so that I would be inspired to improve my own garden. I joined a Scotland's Garden Scheme Tour, couriered by Mrs Lorimer, on which I made some marvellous Scottish friends. I learnt that in an older country the time scale was different. When visiting one Gothic revival mansion the Scots whispered, "New Rich, only made their money in the 1870s."

The Rainforest Garden. The crushed-brick path is edged with box that encloses a garden of rhododendrons, tree ferns and New Zealand trees. The large tree on the right is a New Zealand red beech (Nothofagus fusca)*, probably planted in Larnach's time. Giant lilies* (Cardiocrinum giganteum) *grow on the left foreground.*

I looked at the area behind the ballroom where, in the nineteenth century, Larnach had planted in the fashion of the time large North American conifers. He may have also planted there the native red beech or tawhai *(Nothofagus fusca)* judging by its size, a more unusual tree in gardens at that time. In the 1920s and 1930s, the Purdies established a 'shrubbery' beneath these trees. By the 1970s, the large old North American conifers were thinning at the tops and dropping their necrotic limbs onto the ballroom roof. Beneath, the shrubbery had evolved into an intertwined tangle of undergrowth in a slow-motion dance as each plant struggled to compete for a share of precious light. An intermittent box hedge survived here and there. Trees worth keeping were the red beech and a broadleaf *Griselinia littoralis.* A cryptomeria and a thujopsis were retained because they gave a feeling of enclosure. To treasure were some tree ferns, *Dicksonia fibrosa* and *D. squarrosa*.

The scruffy North American conifers were felled and the undergrowth cleared. Sophie and Norcombe were a bit upset that their 'Forest of No Return', where they had built their huts, was being demolished. I said, "Don't worry. By the time your children come here to play it will again be a 'Forest of No Return' but with better trees."

ABOVE: *A rata* (Metrosideros carminea) *finally reaches the top of a five-metre tree fern. Fortunately, I had the forethought to plant this in the 1970s, as it took 20 years to flower.* OPPOSITE: *The perfumed* Rhododendron maddenii *ssp* maddenii *in front of a young rimu. A broadleaf* (Griselinia littoralis) *arches over the path.*

The podocarps, rimu, totara, kahikatea, matai and miro were established. Trees of ancient lineage native to other areas of New Zealand were also planted, including rewarewa, tanekaha (the celery pine) and a kauri. The kauri is a native of the north of New Zealand but fossils of its ancestors have been found in the south. Structural timbers in the Castle are of kauri, as are the veranda floors and the handrails of the staircases. Panelling above the dado in the foyer and in the main stairwell is of plain and mottled kauri. Larnach's original bed in the master bedroom is of bird's eye kauri with specially selected markings, as are the wardrobe and chest in the same room. On the dado in the foyer, behind the ebony spindles, rewarewa is used as a decorative band of characteristically speckled wood.

I planted a rewarewa tree the day my father died. Each year on the eleventh hour of the eleventh day of the eleventh month my children and I gather in the rainforest by this tree to remember my father and his experiences as a soldier in World War I. He was in the Battle of the Somme and at other places in France and many times thought that he would die. His friends had been killed. Then he was posted as a flautist to the New Zealand Divisional Orchestra, and became a member of the original Kiwi Concert Party. When peace was declared he was in France in the village of Beaucourt. He decided then that one day he would have a house and a family and he would call his home 'Beaucourt'.

In my memory I could picture the bush at Morere Springs. When I was three years old my mother took my sister and me to stay at this spa north of Napier. I remembered my mother giving ration coupons to the dining room waitress, issued because of the war, and I also remembered the sherry trifle. Daily we walked to the bathhouses in the bush through the famous pure stands of nikau palms with criss-crossing leaves which formed a lattice pattern. I remember looking up and down at the circular tracery of the abundant tree ferns. They looked like Victorian lace doilies. I decided to recreate these remembered patterns, evocative of our New Zealand bush.

The nikau palms which I planted in the rainforest died because this area is a frost pocket. Disappointed by this failure I focused on the tree ferns which I planted on either side of the long box-edged walk, adding various *Cyathea* spp. to the *Dicksonia* spp. that were already there. *Cyathea smithii*, the soft tree fern, and *C. dealbata*, are both native to the Otago Peninsula. The silver underside of the *C. dealbata* frond is New Zealand's national emblem, displayed on a black background on uniforms worn by our sporting teams. Mamaku (*C. medullaris*), our largest tree fern, has elegant curving black stipes with feathered fronds. The emerging curled up fern leaf, or koru, unfurls upwards then arches back. Koru in Maori means new life. As one frond dies, another grows, symbolising lineage, or whakapapa, and the passing on of life, information and resources from one generation to the next. As the koru unfolds, reaching towards the light, it

signifies the spiritual values of new beginnings, a striving for perfection, rebirth and hope for the future.

Rick Darke, then the curator of plants at Longwood Garden in Pennsylvania, America, stayed here and asked me to send him spores of the mamaku for Longwood. Counterpointed by sharply clipped box, luxuriant lacy fern fronds surround and sweep over the 40-metre walk, the patterns repeating against the sky. Mountain cabbage trees *(Cordyline indivisa)* are planted on either side of the end path forming a lusty avenue. *Metrosideros carminea*, the scarlet climbing rata, was planted to grow up an established tree fern about 25 years ago. Taking 20 years to flower, it now makes a spectacular show each November.

Scotland was again a source of inspiration when, in 2004, I visited Inverewe on Scotland's west coast. There, I saw massed celmisias and ourisias that were the best plantings of these New Zealand natives that I had ever seen. On my return, I promptly installed three copper sentinels with misting nozzles at the top along the shaded bed immediately behind the ballroom. In the humid area created, I strive to emulate the ourisias of Inverewe. In this fog garden I have also planted fork ferns *(Tmesipteris* spp.*)*, Prince of Wales feathers, hen and chicken ferns and kidney ferns. The fork fern is a relict plant, thought to be a relative of the first plants to grow leaf-like structures. In my new rainforest garden, I also planted *Dracophyllum* spp. of various kinds, and these New Zealand grass trees now assume postures from Dr Seuss. These are my New Zealand plants.

But I am an acquisitive gardener, so plants other than natives add to the ambience of the rainforest garden. Large-leafed rhododendrons are splendid foliage plants. One I acquired as *R. macabeanum* was grown from seed collected from the Dunedin Botanic Gardens. It grew to a very large umbrella before having its first flower. There was only one, flowering right at the top like a knob on the umbrella. We admired this plant's sense of humour for popping up a flower on top like this, but the flower proclaimed it to be – in the plant world we are polite about these things – a hybrid. *R. macabeanum* had crossed with the *R. gigantum* next door, the miscreant

LEFT: *Mountain cabbage trees* (Cordyline indivisa) *poised like Balinese dancers.* RIGHT: *The whorl of new growth, or koru, of a mamaku* (Cyathea medullaris)*, or black tree fern.*

being the bee not the plants. Now, a very large tree with hybrid vigour, this rhododendron makes up in enthusiasm for what it lacks in genetic purity.

Rhododendrons of the Maddennii subsection are grown for their perfume and lily-like flowers. Also *Rhododendron* 'Cornubia', a favourite in Dunedin gardens, is cherished because it cheers late winter days with its luminous red trusses. In summer, the air is again perfumed by the giant lilies *Cardiocrinum giganteum*. These then form seed heads like standard candelabra. Some giant lilies planted where we had had a fire heap developed bulbs the size of footballs and flower heads almost like lighthouses. This was because of the potash in the ashes. We now feed the bulbs after flowering with a fertiliser high in potash to encourage the magnificent blooms.

Perennial plants behind the ballroom include *Veratrum nigrum*, which is worth garden space for its pleated leaves alone, but it also bears strange almost black flower spikes more than a metre high. I saw *Lobelia tupa* growing in Chile near Valdivia, which has a climate similar to ours, and I have planted a great swathe for its dark red flowers. In Chile this plant is pollinated by hummingbirds and here it is much loved by bellbirds.

The long walk required a focus for the end. Figures in the garden from Sir John Tenniel's drawings illustrating Lewis Caroll's *Alice's Adventures in Wonderland* intrigue our visitors, so I decided to augment this theme with a Queen of Hearts Throne. Stu Robbie, the cabinetmaker, made a template of plywood first and this was mounted in situ to give an idea of scale. A lovely big pink heart in fretwork graces the back of this oversize chair. The completed throne is an unqualified success with visitors to the garden and is constantly photographed with lovers, grannies and children of all ages on its roomy seat. We are surprised that people from many different cultures grasp the literary reference.

Podocarps are long lived but slow-growing survivors. The kahikatea, rimu, totara, matai and miro that I have planted are not yet very tall. Our great-great-grandchildren may see their eventual splendour. This planting, a small amendment for the damage done by the settlers to the Otago Peninsula's pristine rainforest, connects the distant past with the future.

ABOVE: *The seldom seen* Veratrum nigrum, *with dark flowers and pleated leaves.*
RIGHT: Lobelia tupa *is from Chile but is beloved by New Zealand bellbirds for its nectar.*

CHAPTER EIGHT

Achieving Clarity

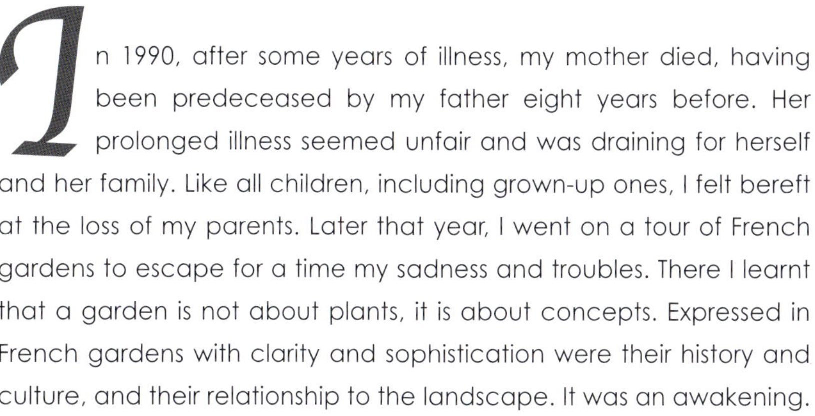

In 1990, after some years of illness, my mother died, having been predeceased by my father eight years before. Her prolonged illness seemed unfair and was draining for herself and her family. Like all children, including grown-up ones, I felt bereft at the loss of my parents. Later that year, I went on a tour of French gardens to escape for a time my sadness and troubles. There I learnt that a garden is not about plants, it is about concepts. Expressed in French gardens with clarity and sophistication were their history and culture, and their relationship to the landscape. It was an awakening.

I travelled for a month with a group of Americans on a Pacific Horticulture Tour. We looked at art and gardens and I learnt how to contemplate gardens as if they were art. There were specific lessons that stay with me today, and the gardens became a part of my consciousness.

We all try to capitalise on what we are given in our garden site, but none of us could be as lucky as Louis XIV's second wife, the Marquise de Maintenon, who was given an aqueduct by him for the bottom of her garden. The Château de Maintenon dates back to the Middle Ages and was purchased in 1674 for the Marquise, who at the time was the king's secret wife and went by the name of Françoise d'Aubigne. The aqueduct was built by Vauban, Louis XIV's famous military engineer, to carry the waters of the River Eure to Versailles, but was never fully completed. In the late seventeenth century, the Marquise de Maintenon embellished and repositioned the Château so that it faced the aqueduct.

The labernum pergola dripping with golden racemes frames the Castle in late spring.

The great seventeenth-century French designer Andre Le Nôtre was responsible for the garden around the château and his design dramatised the overwhelming presence of the aqueduct. The massive structure was reflected in a huge pool that he constructed in front of the château which was designed to be seen from the upstairs windows of the château.

A waterless and barren cliff face in Monaco, drenched by sun, does not seem a promising site for a garden. However, Monaco's Prince Albert I called in Louis Notari, a civil engineer, to answer the challenge. He harnessed the difficulties of the site to his advantage to create La Jardin Exotique de Monaco. Footbridges were built, rocks moved and soil brought in. The garden was opened in 1933 and now over half a million people visit it annually. I had to overcome vertigo to explore this garden high above Monte Carlo where the strange shapes of the xerophytes that are its mainstay are outlined against the sky. It made me wonder about the courage of the gardeners who had to stake cacti on a cliff face. Prince Albert's garden is a triumph over adversity.

As at Larnach Castle, the garden at the Château de Courances in France has been lost and restored twice. Perhaps some gardens have their own destiny and we are just their servants. Courances has survived for 300 years despite hard times. It is now the home of the de Ganay family, who bought the château and garden in 1872 after it had been abandoned for 42 years. The de Ganays restored and maintained the property. 'Courances' in French means 'running waters' and there are ten springs on the property. Water gushes out of stone dolphin heads called 'gueulards', into a serene composition of rectangular ponds. There is moving water and still water, but no mechanical devices are used. This typical *parc a la francais* is attributed to Le Nôtre and was created at the end of the seventeenth century. Ponds are in the open in sunlight, in the shade among trees, or lined by hedges and tall trees. Each pond captures the light, and the theme of light upon the water is expressed in variety. Some ponds have weirs, some swans and some fountains, but most are still. At Courances, as in many gardens by Le Nôtre, *allées* of trees lead the eye into the distant landscape. In other Le Nôtre gardens, I saw how he opened up the central vista, established open space around châteaux and achieved a sense of scale, balance and proportion.

At La Chevre d'Or, a garden created by M and Mme Pierre Champlin, we were told that the structure is what counts – anything else can be put in later. They had planted little trees and watched them grow. "Plant for a hundred years," Mme Champlin said.

La Columbieres, a tragically ruined garden above Menton near the Italian border, is the only

---

ABOVE: *Enjoying La Jardin Exotique de Monaco.* OPPOSITE, CLOCKWISE FROM TOP: *Vaux-le-Vicomte, a garden designed by Le Vau, Le Brun and Le Nôtre. The trees were pruned to lead the eye into the vista, a concept I brought home with me. A composition of trees, hedges, lawn and a reflection pond at Courances. La Columbieres – light shines on a pool seen down a dark alley of cypress trees.*

extant garden of Ferdinand Bac, a designer during the early twentieth century. I was captivated by its overwhelming ambience. Bac derived his inspiration from the Italian and Persian gardens of the past. He said that the composition of La Columbieres was a "submission to the majestic panorama". He created frames to capture garden views. Bac said that in his imagination he could see a garden like a cathedral, in which the idea of infinity would be the first thing to establish by means of spacious vistas. Looking down a long dark *allée* of Italian cypress, I glimpsed the light reflected on a pool.

I come home to face larger issues that loomed in my life. Our marriage had become untenable. Barry wanted financial freedom and selling his capital share of Larnach Castle would enable him to pursue his other interests, but I wanted to hold onto the dream. So the next year, we finally decided to go our different ways. Norcombe and Sophie, of their own volition, became my new partners in the Castle adventure. We bought Barry's share of the mortgaged Castle over a period of years – it had been valued for the separation at 16 times what we had paid for it in 1967. It was an emotionally and financially difficult time for our small family.

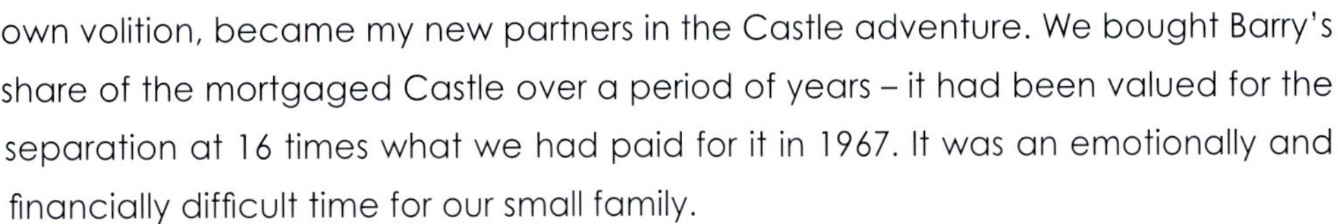

We determined to continue restoring the Castle and its surrounds. While many systems had been somewhat improved over our 24 years of travail, the toilet building was grossly inadequate, the electric wiring dangerously faulty, the plumbing unreliable and the Lodge needed rebuilding. To pay interest and capital on various loans we had to improve the facilities so that we could enlarge the business. To achieve growth we borrowed more money until we owed more that we were worth. We worked very long hours at the beck and call of the paying guests, while the very real spectre of financial failure hung over us. We could so easily have lost all we had worked for.

Despite our troubles I decided to make a bold gesture and redesign the grounds as seen to the west from the tower and the main Castle doors. I poured my thoughts and sorrows of this time, and my will to go forward, into the new landscaping at the front of the Castle. To achieve my ideal I put into practice the lessons I had learned on my latest trip overseas. I would sweep away what we had, retaining only the central Raised Lawn and newly built pergola, and restructure the grounds to achieve the clarity and purpose that I had admired in France.

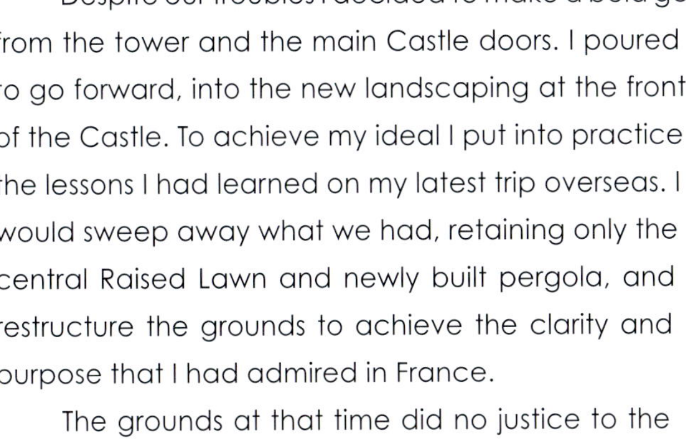

The grounds at that time did no justice to the historic building, nor to the splendid surrounding landscape. The layout was sideways to the axis of the powerful and symmetrical architecture. The large space in front of the Castle was successful,

open to the sky with no distractions, and the Raised Lawn balanced the mass of the Castle. Beyond this lawn and across the axis, the Purdies had planted a lonicera hedge. Mrs Purdie told me that the other side of the hedge was where they grew their spuds.

But the Raised Lawn was tired, the edges had slumped and much of the surrounding stone wall had crumbled away. The lonicera hedge had billowed and flopped. It wobbled its way across the view. We had cut it back and given it a feed but lonicera is not a good choice for a taller hedge, because it is not strong enough to hold itself upright. We had replaced the rotted and collapsed lath tunnel with a metal pergola. This spacious structure took its design from the Gothic arch at the front entrance of the Castle. Looking back from within, it framed the Castle in a wonderful way, but in the opposite direction it led to a hole in the ground.

An even larger hole bore testimony to where a previous owner had excavated for a swimming pool, which was never completed. Views through the sides of the pergola were of the surrounding car park, which sloped left to right. Beyond the hedge, but visible from the upper windows of the Castle and tower, was a large car park edged with gorse bushes, self-sown holly, blackberry and various woody weeds. Stored in the car park were heaps of gravel and stone, a boat, a few old cars, a couple of early Fordson tractors and a miscellany of other larger artefacts. A 50-metre-high background of shelter trees blocked any further view that there may have been.

The time had come to clean up my act, which I planned to do stage by stage, moving outwards from the Castle.

At this time, we were approached by a foreign film crew. They wanted to do a fashion shoot of horses and riders doing jumps on our Raised Lawn. We agreed they could do this if they paid to reinstate the lawn which would surely be damaged during the shoot. Jim Guest, our lawyer, drew up

the contract. They were to pre-pay fees and expenses including the reinstatement of the lawn. The film crew moved into the Lodge. Beautifully dressed riders were filmed doing the jumps in the bright spring sunshine. Then it began to rain. It rained and it rained. The lawn turned into a quagmire.

Unable to film, the crew got grumpy; they just wanted to finish their work and go home. Every morning Sophie cooked them fried-egg sandwiches for breakfast, because that is what they had asked for. Then spring came again with a glorious day. The beautifully dressed riders reappeared and started doing their jumps, but we still had not received our pre-payment. Norcombe rang Jim Guest.

"What should we do?" he asked, explaining the situation.

"Go out there and ask them for it," Jim instructed.

I took some deep breaths and bravely Norcombe and I went forth for the verbal joust, amidst the pantomime on the lawn. I knew I had to retrieve what was owed. I went to the head man, reminded him of our contract, of our beautiful setting and of all the fried egg sandwiches that they had had for breakfast. Through his interpreter, he said that we were questioning his honour. It was even worse because I was a woman. I said that it would be a pity if they had to leave with only half the film in the can. He got cash out of a bum bag that was strapped to his midriff and gave us a wad of notes. After checking and receipting, this same wad of notes was put into a bank bag and handed on to the contractor for the lawn.

"This is not the usual way I do business," he said.

"Don't worry about it," I replied. "We will all do our book work later."

The foreign film crew left New Zealand owing another contractor $20,000. We got a nice new lawn. Fresh soil was brought in, the grass resown, the edges raised and the surrounding dry stone wall was rebuilt.

OPPOSITE, TOP: *On returning from France, I realised what a mess we had back home. The view from the Castle tower with the big hole in the ground to the right of the picture.*
OPPOSITE, BELOW: *The laburnum pergola, which I had built a few years previously, terminated in a hole in the ground which was bridged by two logs. Where was my view?*
THIS PAGE TOP: *Norcombe and a friend by the reflection pool. The yew hedge had just been planted.*
RIGHT: *Ewen Cadzow prunes the fastigiate yew as part of the whole clean-up process at the front of the Castle.*

The Castle faced west and to create a view on the axis we decided to risk cutting a narrow glimpse through the forbidding dark belt of shelter trees. To mitigate wind throw, this was done over a period of years as the remaining shelter was essential. The last of the great 50-metre trees on the line of the axis were felled by the arborist Ewen Cadzow. Before he had fast footed it back up the hill to check if he had dropped the right trees, a visitor was already filming the view. It was a triumph – Larnach's original vision was revealed. Across the Otago Harbour 300 metres below was a vista of Dunedin with Saddle Hill's outstanding presence beyond. This landmark, which rises steeply from the surrounding plain to 1,214 metres, is in the line of the axis, and perfectly centred. The pergola arches framed this compelling view. In summer, it is backlit by the setting sun.

Our foreman, John Murray, had built the central pergola of ten repeating arches. It was planted in laburnum and we waited years before the trees met at the top to create, in flowering season, a tunnel of gold. Then two things happened. One was that the laburnum trees contracted silver leaf disease, and the other was that the wood pigeons ate the flowers and the leaves. We dealt with the silver leaf disease with injections of trichoderma. We now also periodically replace the trees. The wood pigeons we prod in the belly with a long stick, to shoo them away.

In my imagination I saw light on the water. A reflection pool at the end of the pergola would connect the pond on the Raised Lawn to the harbour below. At the end of the pergola, the ground fell steeply away. Fill was brought in to raise the ground and the central area was compacted. I drew up the specifications for a rectangular pond and its position in relation to the base of the pergola. A contractor was given the specifications and he built the pond and went on his way. Norcombe looked at it from the tower. The pond was not in the middle and it was a rhomboid not a rectangle.

We thought about this for a while and decided that you can't have a straight Castle and a crooked pond. The contractor was asked back to rebuild the pond. We refused to pay the large account for the work until the pond was corrected.

"I won't rebuild it and I'll sue you in Court for the money," the contractor said.

TOP: *A kereru, or native wood pigeon, feasts on the laburnum.* ABOVE: *A Pekin duck has found a home for its family at the base of one of the yew trees on the Raised Lawn. The ducks are the most photographed feature of the entire garden.* OPPOSITE: *Soil was brought in to raise the lawn at the side of the laburnum pergola. The newly pruned yew tree is to the right of the Castle.*

We bought in another contractor who broke up the pond, which also leaked, and who built a new one as had been specified. The first contractor made good his threat and took us to Court. In presenting his case to the Court, the hapless contractor proudly produced some photographs. He said that he had been to the Castle within the last few days to take them surreptitiously, which was true because we knew nothing about them. He proudly proclaimed that the photographs showed that there could not be a straighter, truer or more professionally built structure.

In cross-examination, our lawyer enjoyed himself, taking some time to put to the witness a series of photographs taken by Norcombe.

"Do you recognise where these were taken?" he asked.

"Yes, it's the reflecting pool at the Castle."

"And can you positively identify the pool as being the one built by you?"

"Yes, that's definitely it," the contractor confidently asserted.

"Just look ahead to the remaining photographs . . . do you see men working on the pool?"

"Yes."

"What are they doing in the photographs?"

"Well, they appear to be demolishing it."

"Would you agree that they are in fact well into the task of demolishing it?"

"Yes."

"Does that make you think any differently about the photographs you have produced to the Court?"

"I suppose the pool has been replaced," he admitted.

He lost his case.

Then the rules and regulations people from the Town Hall came and stuck a ruler in the pond. It was eight centimetres too deep, which meant, officially, it was a swimming pool, and under the safety laws had to be fenced. So we emptied it, poured some more concrete in the bottom to turn the swimming pool into a reflection pond within the regulations. It was painted off-black to obscure its depth and enhance reflections. As I look into the pond 'through a glass darkly' I do not dwell on its genesis.

The demented old lonicera hedge was dumped in a paddock with a digger by Dave Jensen, the farmer next door. We contemplated the amended landscape. At ground level there were a few things that had been revealed that we didn't want to see – the car parks and the changes in level and the generally scruffy surrounds. I decided that the central area needed to sweep the eye from the Castle and the Raised Lawn into the view.

Architecture was required – green, grand and compelling. William Fulton, a young landscape architect, drew a plan for hedges that led out to the view. A green 'room' around the reflection pond was to be crenellated to echo the tower. Most of the parking facilities had to be shifted to other parts of the property. Norcombe thought that the sloping ground on either side of the pergola should be levelled. On the side that was lowered we hit igneous rock. Dave Jensen tackled this with a hired

pneumatic drill but the rock resisted and broke the bit. To build up the other side we emptied our cellar of old television sets, fridges and freezers. These and other non-functioning bits of machinery were buried under truckloads of new soil. In a few thousand years, archaeologists might have an interesting time retrieving it all.

I had been collecting self-sown yew trees from under the shelter belts and had grown them on for the Green Room. The hedged walls were planted and, unsure of the exact proportions of the room, I had the yews shifted several times. Norcombe and Greg, the lads planting these trees, became profoundly irritated by my vacillations.

For the hedges that swept into the view I had a better idea. I would spray the line first with Roundup. I didn't quite like the line when I saw it from the tower so I sprayed it again leaving two brown marks in the grass. Norcombe asked why I didn't work out a line by cutting it in the grass with a mower. We would then not have to re-sow the grass. When they grew, these hedges of macrocarpa disguised the banks that were created when the central area was levelled.

A floor was created for the Green Room. New soil with sand was laid, levelled and grass seed sown. Having no foreign film crew to sponsor this landscaping, Sophie, Norcombe and I tilled the ground and sowed the grass ourselves. A very unusual rainstorm of 20 centimetres followed and water running

down the slope to the Green Room turned the floor into waves. It was re-levelled and re-sown. Newly sown grass to the side of the pergola turned brown and died, as did streaks of grass down the bank. It turned out that the beach sand supplied had a salt content, which became acid when mixed with the lawn fertiliser. These lawns were washed and re-sown.

We planted groups of cabbage trees (*Cordyline australis*) either side of the pergola to give a sense of place. We worked at a feverish pitch because (such excitement!) the garden was to be featured for the *Palmers' Garden Show* with Maggie Barry. We spruced up the garden in every direction for the camera's critical eye. Ready-lawn was laid in the pergola for the all-important interview. Came the day and the weather held. Maggie was fabulous, as always, and so professional. It was spring and we were filmed walking down the pergola, framed by the laburnum which was freshly breaking into new leaf. I spoke of the beauty of green and wore a green dress, to help make my point. Our garden, the Reflection Pool and new landscaping was shown on television. My brother called just after the show.

"What did you think?" I asked.

He said, "You looked fat."

Gothic arches were trained in the macrocarpa hedge, repeating the design of the pergola and Castle entrance. The macrocarpa arches are at a 45-degree angle to the pergola. A box hedge, the windowsill to the vista from the Green Room, developed a fungal disease. It was removed with regret and *Pittosporum tenuifolium* 'Golf Ball' was planted as a replacement. The gardeners and I now prefer the pittosporum, which is kept clipped into balls.

OPPOSITE, TOP: *I drew the arches for the hedge on this photograph with a green felt pen. It took ten years for the macrocarpa arches to grow and form.* OPPOSITE: *Hedges and a pergola lead to the Green Room in the background.* ABOVE: *The Green Room with the Reflection Pool.*

So many people photographed the vista either back to the Castle or out to the sea from the same position that they didn't just wear out the grass, they actually made a hole in the ground. We placed a slab of polished basalt on the spot where the photographers stand.

For an exhibition, a sculpture of Takaka Hill marble, glistening white with faint green striations, was placed beyond the Reflection Pool by the sculptor Ray Ansin. He called it 'Spiritual Waka. Boat carrying the Spirit over the Waters of Time'. On a black basalt base, it floats a little above the pool. Both the sculpture and its reflected image are framed by the arch. It was purchased as it was felt that the 'Spiritual Waka' had found its home.

Fifteen years on from my inspirational visit to France, the hedges and arches have matured to lend visual strength to the scene. As I write this, a wedding service is taking place in the Green Room by the Reflection Pool. For these people, and for others, it will remain a memorable place. From this yew-hedged room, the Castle and sparkling fountain are framed by the pergola. Surrounding trees soar to the infinite sky. They frame the vista to the sea and the world beyond. The pool reflects the light. Images of the trees, the sky and the Spiritual Waka are captured in its mysterious depths. With the distillation and enhancement of nature's works, we have created a green cathedral.

LEFT: *Jacoba Wyeth and Simon Sidey exchange wedding vows in the Green Room. Jacoba is wearing a dress designed by Dunedin designer Tanya Carlson. Simon is an arborist who had pruned the trees in the vista that week just in time for his wedding.* ABOVE: *The City of Dunedin as seen through the end of the laburnum arch. Saddle Hill is perfectly framed in the background.*

CHAPTER NINE

Dare I Mention My Love Affair with Rhododendrons?

I come from Napier which has hot, dry summers and limey soils where rhododendrons refuse to grow, so I was amazed by the colourful spectacle of the rhododendrons that transform Dunedin each spring. Cleverly named – for the northern hemisphere – pink *Rhododendron* 'Christmas Cheer' enliven gardens from the shortest day, soon joined by the acid-yellow of 'Chrysomanicum'. Voluminous bushes of scarlet 'Cornubia', dripping with blood-red blooms, are a celebration all over Dunedin as winter days lengthen.

Then tree-like *R. arboreum*, with trusses of pink, red, crimson or white, complements the Victorian mansions of Dunedin's old hill suburbs. For six weeks in spring, there is a crescendo of colour. Plants laden with flowers of blue, cream and yellow, purple, scarlet and every expression of pink from blush to cerise, jostle for attention in a surfeit of bloom. Many are perfumed, and the air is heavy with scent.

Rhododendrons are superbly displayed at the Dunedin Botanic Garden and in Glenfalloch nearby, a valley garden in Macandrew

ABOVE: *I admire a* Rhododendron grande. RIGHT: *Colourful rhododendrons below the Lodge. This is the garden as it was about 1990.*

Bay. My head decided that another large rhododendron garden was not required, but my heart led me where I had decided not to go. I plunged into their riches. I was seduced; besotted by their sumptuous complexity. I became an avid collector.

R. augustinii embraced my attention, with its flowers like blue butterflies clustered along the stems. Its New Zealand bred hybrid, 'Ilam Violet', was a deeper shade of blue. Exquisite pink bells hovered all over compact, mounded *R. williamsianum*. *R. nuttallii* had the largest corollas, lily-shaped, cream with golden throats the texture of parchment. The new bullate foliage was dark plum-purple. Its sister *R. lindleyi*'s lily flowers were delicate porcelain-white, sometimes flushed with pink. They were scented, as was 'Mi Amor', the sensational hybrid between them. On 'Loderi' rhododendrons, amplitudinous trusses weighed down the branches.

Deciduous *R. schlippenbachii* had dainty apple-blossom flowers on naked wood, and 'Trewithen Orange' was a new colour break, with flowers the shade of fresh carrot juice. *Cinnabarinum* var. *roylei* has hanging, trumpet-shaped, plum-coloured flowers. Oh the diversity, the splendour! Waxen, scarlet bells decorated *R. thomsonii*, the flowers complemented by rounded glaucous foliage like blue pennies. Its Dunedin bred hybrid 'Marquis of Lothian' had larger, crushed-strawberry bells in loose trusses, a signature plant in Dunedin gardens including, of course, mine.

Aristocrats of nature, large-leafed rhododendrons of the *R. grande* and *R. falconeri* alliances, compelled with their huge flowers, which would be *outré* but for their refinement of form and noble stance. I had to have these, and *R. formosum* (meaning beautiful), nutmeg-scented 'Princess Alice', and 'Hummingbird', 'Chikor', 'Red Dazzle', 'Scarlet Wonder,' 'Blue River' and 'One Thousand Butterflies'. I indulged, blind to the attributes of other plants of the world. This insanity lasted a full 20 years.

Then rhododendrons took me on a journey that changed me. The last decades of the twentieth century were an exhilarating time for rhododendron collectors because from the late 1970s China was tentatively opening its doors to Western visitors, after being closed since Chairman Mao's Red Revolution in 1948. I had first travelled to China in 1981 on an Otago University study tour. The Cultural Revolution was still an open wound. Chinese people talked to us freely then, some with quiet acceptance and irony, others with a compelling need to share their pain.

In May, 1993, an opportunity arose to visit China's Yunnan province, the epicentre of rhododendrons. Escorted by Chinese botanists we were to travel to the wild places made famous by the plant explorers George Forrest, Joseph Rock and Frank Kingdon Ward. This tour was organised by Pukeiti Rhododendron Trust and led by Lynn Bublitz, a great plantsman from New Plymouth.

Our party of 32 flew out of Hong Kong from the old Kai Tak airport on the Chinese airline Dragonair, the flight path seeming to pass between the tall buildings. With a name like that, I was waiting for the Boeing to breathe great balls of fire. We landed at Kunming, the capital of Yunnan, and were met by Tony Ji Xiangsheng, who was our guide and friend in China. He took us to meet our hosts at the Kunming Institute of Botany, where we were given innumerable cups of tea.

Yunnan is the wild west of China, infested with bandits and ruled by warlords early in the twentieth century, then occupied by the Japanese. It was freed during World War II by Americans who flew "over the hump", as they called the Himalaya Mountains which separate India from Yunnan. In 1949 Yunnan became part of China and closed its doors to the West. Twenty-four ethnic groups people Yunnan, each with their own language, traditions and dress.

OPPOSITE: *A few rhododendrons survived my decision to remove the rhododendron garden. Beyond, the South Seas Garden and the harbour.* ABOVE: *A large-leafed rhododendron is taken away on a trailer on the start of a journey to a new home.*

CHAPTER TEN

South Seas Garden

The hidden landscape was revealed. In 1996 and 1997, we took out the great dark wall of macrocarpa trees which hid the surrounding landscape from the Lodge and the Stable Drive. I used to skid down the bank and stand on a tree stump to take in the beautiful view which floated, resplendent, around and below.

From 300 metres above, I could look down on the harbour to the indented coastline, towards the heads and the Pacific Ocean beyond. Opposite was Port Chalmers, with its steepled church where Captain Robert Scott worshipped before his fateful journey to the South Pole. The land rose steeply from the harbour, which had been formed by a volcanic eruption. Mount Cargill, which Maori named Kapukataumauhaka (the sleeping princess), loomed at 676 metres on the opposite side. Harbour Cone, a fumerole, was a distinctive symmetrical landmark on the peninsula, beyond which was Taiaroa Head where penguins and royal albatrosses nest and breed.

The beautiful view is a pageant of changing light. The water glitters and dazzles in the sun on sharp clear days and, when clouds are reflected, the harbour glows like silk until scudded by wind. It then turns grey and non-reflective. Storms move across the landscape in the dark light of winter days. Sometimes we are completely enveloped in sea mist, the world hidden from us; then we feel lost in space and time. Or we might hover over the fog if it settles on the harbour, in our own

The South Seas Garden. The spikey flowers on the left are Aciphylla glaucescens. *The long panicles with pink bracts hanging over the garden below the cabbage tree* (Cordyline australis) *are from* Beschorneria yuccoides.

white world, shared only with Mount Cargill and Harbour Cone. Except when the wretched nor'easter blows straight down the harbour and into your face, the tableau is beautiful in every mood.

I wanted visitors to the Castle to be similarly enthralled and to share this sublime panorama.

I decided to build a belvedere in the same position as the tree stump where I had often stood. To reach the belvedere from above or below, we needed to build a connecting staircase. At the other end from the envisaged staircase, a path went down through the garden, but it led nowhere, so visitors had to double back. The base of the new staircase would rise from the end of that existing path and climb to the Stable Drive, creating a loop for people exploring the garden.

I drew a concept sketch of the staircase, incorporating a level sitting-out area, and linking the belvedere to an existing viewing platform that our foreman, John Murray, had built some years previously on the Stable Drive. I thought of the staircase as having two movements. The first floated around from the viewing platform down to the belvedere, then curved through greenery to the ground. Movement two of the staircase was to be set into the hillside, strong and monumental as is the surrounding landscape. The style of belvedere was inspired by one I had photographed at the top of the cable car at Valparaiso in Chile.

OPPOSITE: *The view looking across the Otago Harbour to Port Chalmers framed by the white kaka beak (*Clianthus puniceus *'Albus').* TOP: *The belvedere with steps on a scale commensurate with the size of the garden and the strength of the landscape.* ABOVE, CLOCKWISE FROM LEFT: *The draughtsman's plan of the first flight and belvedere, with my drawings of the lower steps superimposed on the survey drawing. My drawing of part of the lower steps. My sketch of the planting plan for part of the South Seas Garden.*

Mike Sowman, an architectural draughtsman, was engaged to prepare building plans of the first floating flight and the belvedere. He calculated that it would take 68 steps with risers of 175 millimetres to negotiate the steep slope, from the path at the bottom to the viewing platform at the top. The logistical exercise was to fit in all these steps. A structural engineer was consulted and he custom designed curved metal stringers which were cast so that my dream of a staircase floating up to the belvedere and into the vista could come true. It was the very devil to build and fit, but there it is now, sometimes quite crowded with visitors enjoying the view.

A building permit was not required for the big steps in the hillside. I drew up the plans myself without the hassles of regulations and middlemen. Helen Dillon, the famous gardener from Dublin in Ireland, had suggested that I build and plant bigger and bolder as befitted our powerful landscape. To achieve the massive look I sought, I had the timber specially milled. I used the American landscaper Thomas Church's formula of 'twice the riser plus the tread equals 26', to create beauty of flow. The big bottom step is 3.6 metres long, then the steps gently curve and taper as they rise up. All these design facets were ruses to invite visitors to climb up the steep steps to the belvedere.

None of this was easy. It never is. John Murray helped me to calculate the angles of the steps to achieve the curve I wanted, and the building firm Stevenson and Williams made and bolted on the modifications. Glen Coster, a landscaper, set the bottom of the massive timber flight of steps solidly into concrete, and then the steps took off up into the air and had to be held up by concrete piles. We had to take it on faith and trust in Mike's calculations that the solid steps of the second movement would meet up with the floating flight of the first movement, which the builders had started from the top.

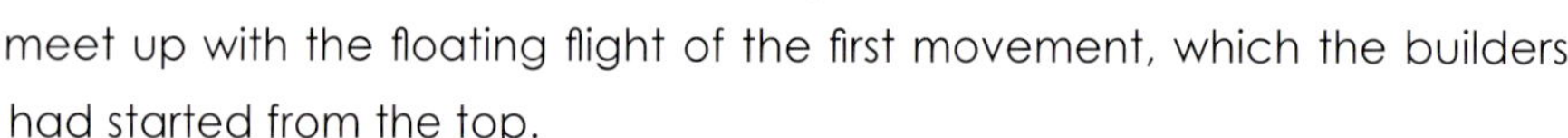

The shape of the hillside was modified with coarse aggregate that was shifted up the hill on a hired moving belt. Glen built stone retaining walls to hold this in place. Large planter boxes were built at the sides of the big top steps to tie them physically and visually into the hill. Oh hooray! The steps all met.

To invigorate the bland hillside, it was re-contoured and installations were built using the large igneous rocks which are the peninsula's natural treasures. Each of the boulders, which were collected from a neighbouring farm and laid first along the Stable Drive for contemplative study,

---

TOP: *Greg, the excavator driver, deftly places a rock.* ABOVE: *Glen and I build the prototype of the rock formation with plastic milk crates.* OPPOSITE: *Otago Harbour from the drive to the Stable. In the foreground, the sculptural silhouettes of the juvenile form of lancewoods* (Pseudopanax crassifolius).

was given a number or name. A prototype of the formation was built on site out of plastic milk crates and it was studied from every angle. Then the design was drawn, rock by rock, on paper. An excavator came down a purpose built ramp to carry in and place the rocks, most of which weighed over a tonne. Greg, the driver, did this elegantly and quickly.

"I am so used to it," he said. "This machine is like my hand, you see."

The rhododendrons were going, then gone. What was I to do with my new empty garden? It was a garden with a view of the harbour and hills, with glimpses of the Pacific Ocean. It had to speak of the sea and use plants from islands and coastal places, planted to flow like the surrounding land forms, with curves following the coastline below. My thoughts drifted to islands where I had been. Wasn't Otago Peninsula almost an island? Such was the genesis of the South Seas Garden.

I had been to the Chatham Islands on a tour led by Gordon Collier. We flew southeast from Wellington for two hours, and while on the plane we were served a Devon tea of freshly baked scones with jam and cream. When we landed we adjusted our watches forward by 45 minutes, as the Chatham Islands are the first place in the world to see the new day.

The first settlers on the Chathams were the Moriori, people of the same Polynesian stock as the Maori, who sailed from New Zealand between 400 – 600 years ago. Moriori had their own dialect and culture and lived a peaceful life in harmony with nature, conserving the land which provided their sustenance. They called their islands Rekohu, meaning 'misty skies'. Moriori numbers were decimated, first by the Maori who settled the Chathams in 1832, and then by diseases brought by later European settlers. In 1933, Tommy Solomon, said to be the last full-blooded Moriori, died. Today, there are many Chatham Islanders who are descended from Moriori and who identify themselves as such. Some residents are descended from all of the three racial groups – Moriori, Maori and European – that now live on the islands. Farming and fishing support the economy. In the recent past the islands were over-

fished and the countryside ravaged by farming, burning and feral pigs. Nowadays, the islanders value conservation, as did the Moriori, and there are fishing quotas and land set aside as reserves where the original plant cover is regenerating.

During our visit we spent happy days discovering for ourselves the Chatham's renowned endemic plants, interspersed with picnic lunches and a visit to the local Black Robin Brewery. The Chatham Island forget-me-not (*Myosotidium hortensia*), a megaherb treasured by gardeners, is the signature plant of the islands. Its large shiny cordate leaves are handsome in themselves, but it also has clusters of true blue flowers, like the velvet ones made to decorate old-fashioned ladies' hats. We found it growing in sand along the beach on the landward side of the coastal rocks, where it sometimes received doses of seaweed and the remains of marine life. Nature teaches us a plant's needs for cultivation – for the forget-me-nots, it's excellent drainage with mild moist conditions and a good feed, too.

Growing on peat in an upland bog, *Olearia semidentata* was regenerating in an area fenced off as a reserve. Lavender cineraria-like daisies smothered the grey-leafed shrubs. This plant is well worth growing because it flowers for months, although the only gardens where I have seen it planted, besides mine, are Mount Stewart in Ireland, Tresco Abbey Gardens in the Scilly Isles and Tregwainton in Cornwall. Why isn't it in New Zealand gardens?

OPPOSITE, TOP: *The outlook from the viewing platform above the South Seas Garden before we cut down the macrocarpa trees. Compare this photograph with the one below taken from the same position after the trees were taken out. The Harbour can now be seen from the viewing platform.* ABOVE: *The rare spiral aloe with red-flowered gazanias in the foreground – both are from South Africa. Beyond is the feathery foliage of the Chatham Island* Coxella dieffenbachii *(syn* Aciphylla dieffenbachii*) and the Chatham Island flax.*

When I planted *Olearia semidentata* at the Castle, I took away the soil and replaced it with peat. I planted native grasses on the roots, as I had seen in nature, to keep them cool and dry. Olearias can drop dead at the drop of a hat from phytophthera, a fungus that attacks plant roots. We admired *Olearia chathamica*, which has white daisy flowers with navy discs.

Brachyglottis huntii was found growing near streams. A few of these large, fresh-green-leafed shrubs were in flower, with conical heads of little massed golden sunflowers. The Chatham Island lancewood *(Pseudopanax chathamica)* has wider, flatter leaves than its New Zealand mainland cousins, that are also not toothed.

There was a lack of divaricating plants in the Chathams. Divaricated plants, characteristic of mainland New Zealand, grow like bunched wire netting, with the tender new growth protected inside the plant. This is food for thought for the proponents of the theory that New Zealand juvenile plants evolved divarication to protect them from grazing moa, as the giant flightless birds populated New Zealand but not the Chathams, until becoming extinct about 300 years ago.

Aged and windswept *Olearia traversii*, gnarled into fantastic formations, dwelt on the beach. There were very few young plants because of grazing by livestock. By coastal rocks and on clifftops we saw the Chatham Island flax, which has a wider, softer leaf on a plant that is more chunky than its New Zealand counterpart. 'Silver spear' was the marketing name chosen by the nursery firm Duncan and Davies for a selected form of *Astelia chathamica*. Silvery and spikey, it looks as delicious in gardens as it was to the feral pigs that almost annihilated this striking endemic plant in the Islands. We had to walk eight kilometres, then climb down a cliff, to see plants of any size in the wild, but the good news is that it, too, is regenerating in the fenced reserves.

At the J.M. Barker Hapupu National Historic Reserve was a poignant reminder of the art of the Moriori. On kopi trees were carvings depicting stylised human figures. When the trees age and die, sadly, the carvings will go too. Kopi, so called by the Moriori, are called karaka trees (*Corynocarpus laevigatus*) on the mainland. It is thought that the Moriori brought kopi seeds to plant as a food source in the islands, as they are not distinct from mainland trees.

We drove, then walked for a way to reach the nikau reserve, which was remote and cool. Before us was a crowded stand of palm trees thrusting their bunches of feathered fronds into the sky, soaring above the surrounding trees. Palm trees – oh joy! At a latitude of 44 degrees south, the Chatham Islands' nikaus are the southernmost palms in the world. Recently they had been fenced from stock and there were many young trees. We stretched up to look at the dusky-pink flowers. There were bunches of green berries from the previous year's bloomings, and red berries from the flowers of the year before that. The palms were growing among kopi trees, hoho – the Chatham Island lancewood – and karamu *(Coprosma chathamica)*. In that moment, I realised that these palm trees would grow on Otago Peninsula, which was not, after all, so far away, similarly cool and also subject to salt-laden gales. They would create the ambience I desired of an island in the eternal Pacific and the southern seas.

When I got home I bought five Chatham Island nikau palm trees. They are more robust than the mainland nikau and have broader leaves. Best of all, they had evolved over millions of years to thrive in a cool and windy maritime climate. I had to buy the trees from Auckland because no local nurseryman had ever dreamt of growing these palm trees for the South Island market. The first few palms were planted on the hillside amongst the rhododendrons and – I couldn't believe it – they got sunburnt. The leaves turned brown and shrivelled. How can a palm tree recently arrived from Auckland get sunburnt in Dunedin? It transpired that they had been grown in a shadehouse. The juvenile palm tree evolved to grow in shade, but the mature tree, when it pops through the top of the canopy, develops a cuticle on the frond to protect it from the sun. But the Chatham palms are clever and adaptive. Of course, they have intelligent thoughts and conversations, though we are deficient and don't comprehend them. A juvenile palm planted out in the sun will throw up a new set of leaves coated in the protective cuticle, just as the adult does. It can take a season or two for the plants to replenish the fronds, but they do.

Long ago, in the distant past, there was a great Southern land now termed Zealandia. Over tens of

OPPOSITE: *When I saw these palm trees growing on the Chatham Islands, I knew that I could grow them on the Otago Peninsula.* ABOVE: *From milk crates to this – the completed rock formation.*

millions of years it eroded and disappeared into the sea. The only remnants of this lost subcontinent are New Zealand and its subantarctic islands, New Caledonia, the Chatham Islands and Lord Howe Island. The plant life of these remnants is closely related because it evolved from the same ancient stock. But the islands have been apart for at least 30 million years, a sufficient time for plant life on each island to develop unique characteristics.

In my travels from New Caledonia in the north, to Campbell Island in the deep south, I have seen patterns of plant distribution. There is a sense of seeing the same thing but with subtle differences. The grass tree (*Dracophyllum scoparium*) and our ratas and their relatives spread from New Caledonia to the subantarctic Auckland Islands. Other plants like araucaria, carmichaelia, bulbinella, macropiper and sophora feature here and there. Our kowhai (*Sophora*) is known locally on Lord Howe as *Lignum vitae* (*Sophora howinsula*). Our macropiper becomes the kava plant of tropical islands. New Zealand kauri is from the family Araucariaceae, which includes the Norfolk Island pine (not a pine at all) and the pin colonnaire of New Caledonia. This common heritage from the past is why the plants on top of Mount Gower on Lord Howe Island are most closely related to the plants of New Zealand's North Island,

just as they were eight million years ago. I just had to climb Mount Gower to have a look at them.

With Sophie, I flew from Dunedin to Christchurch to Sydney then back east to Lord Howe Island, which is administered by Australia. Lord Howe Island was to our eyes lushly furnished with house plants. Dense stands of graceful kentia palms, the world's favourite indoor palm, covered much of the lowland. Spreading limbs of the Lord Howe form of the Morton Bay fig, or rubber tree, drop down aerial roots to the ground which grow into new tree trunks. The fig gradually enlarges its territory, creating a shaded forest of only one tree. Stag horn ferns clasp rocks and trunks, and perching orchids create a tropical ambience on a temperate island.

Early one morning, in the dark before sunrise, a small group of us set out with a guide to climb Mount Gower. We walked a long way on coastal boulders, then crossed the face of Mount Lidgbird wearing hard hats and holding a rope. We went through the Erskine Valley and then began a strenuous vertical climb, pulling ourselves up by ropes, which was a new experience for this middle-aged lady.

At the notorious 'get up place', we went up and across a sheer rock face to a knife-edged ridge, where I looked straight down more than 800 metres to the sea. Vertigo overcame me. But I remember in that moment of terror an amazing sight – on the gunmetal cliff above the blue, blue sea, the occasional palm and tree fern clung to life.

We had to go on over a few more humps before we reached the ancient cloud forest. Here there were pygmy trees, none more than four metres high, in a primeval land enveloped in fog and dripping with mosses, orchids and ferns that the moisture supported. There were mountain palms and tree ferns, grass trees and flowering plants of primitive families. We were enclosed in magic misty verdure. In a waterproof metal box was a visitors' book which we signed, then we had lunch among the alpine rose, the scarlet-flowering *Metrosideros nervulosa*. We were quiet, all thinking the same thing; we had climbed up but now we had to climb down.

The island remnants of the lost subcontinent Zealandia – the Chathams, Lord Howe and the Isle of Pines in New Caledonia, where pin colonnaire grew like massed ships' masts, and our New Zealand coasts – were the inspiration for the South Seas Garden at the Castle.

The old shelter belt below the Lodge and the South Seas Garden needed replacing, but not with elephantine macrocarpa, which would grow to block the beautiful view. I had taken the famous and well-travelled plantsman Christopher Brickell and his wife Jeanette along the peninsula and we saw a crimson-flowering pohutukawa with a bellbird feeding on the nectar, which Chris photographed, trembling with excitement. I suddenly saw the pohutukawa through his English eyes as a spectacular and colourful tree that shouts 'New Zealand' out loud. And it would take any salt gale that was thrown its way. So I planted the hillside with pohutakawas (*Metrosideros excelsa*), *M. umbellata* and *M. robusta*, the southern and northern ratas, and hybrids *M.* 'Mistral' and *M.* 'Maungapiko'. Recently, to mark the birth of my granddaughter Charlotte, we planted *M. bartlettii*, a white rata discovered in 1975

The South Seas Garden from the Stable Drive showing the rarely planted golden pingao grass (Desmoschoenus spiralis), *which is a plant of New Zealand's coastal dunes.*

in the Far North of New Zealand near Cape Reinga. Some Norfolk Island pines (*Araucaria heterophylla*) and pin colonnaire (*A. columnaris*) were added to grow to one day frame the view. The area slopes so sharply to the sea that I called it my vertical arboretum.

I was mulching the pohutukawa one February day with help from Caleb Appleton, who was carrying the buckets of compost up and down the hill. Caleb said, "There are whales down there." We watched them as they swam past Quarantine Island right into Broad Bay, black shadows in the water as big as trucks. They were orca, the killer whales, which come each summer to feed on the seal pups at Taiaroa Head. They toss the baby seals up into the air and play with them like a cat with a mouse.

And so I planted the South Seas Garden with plants from islands and coasts, in drifts and groups, repeating patterns from the sea. Pingao, a golden, tangled, ropey grass, *Muehlenbeckia complexa* and the needle-leafed sand-carpeting *Coprosma acerosa*, all from the New Zealand dunes, counterpoint the soft, plumey carrot-leafed *Coxella dieffenbachii* and thrusting Chatham Island flax, both from the Chatham Islands. The *Coxella* has one-metre creamy-yellow flower stems, with male and female flowers on separate plants. The foliage is not barbed and stiff like the mainland speargrass.

I have *Dendrocerus littoralis*, with its large dish-shaped leaves, from Isla Robinson Crusoe, west of Valparaiso. There are spikey *Dietes robinsoniana*, locally called the wedding lily, and *Carmichaela exsul*, both from Lord Howe. Drifts of *Carmichaelia williamsii,* from islands off New Zealand's East Cape, have large moonlight flowers and coarse foliage like seaweed. The felted grey-leafed Marlborough rock daisy *(Pachystegia insignis)* is from the coastal cliffs of Kaikoura. There is a little forest of shortened trees to remind me of the top of Mt Gower.

Silver-foliaged olearias and astelias from the Chathams suggest breaking foam in the sea. The Stephens Island pittosporum provides excellent shelter from the beastliest gales. *Arthropodium cirratum* 'White Knight', first named this way by Diana Howard, is larger that the mainland rengarenga lily, with foliage to a metre and taller flowers. It comes from the Poor Knights Islands.

Coastal ferns are a refreshing green and a textural delight. I collected *Asplenium obtusatum* locally years ago and Fiona, the Castle's head gardener, has bulked it up by divisions. Its shining patent-leather-like leaves contrast with *Asplenium flaccidum* ssp. *haurakiense*, which has threaded leaves like mermaid's hair. Both ferns grow in the open in the sun.

Some plants are there just because they are blue in foliage or flower, linking the garden to the sky and sea. Dainty dwarf agapanthus flower in February and lapis lazuli *Lithodora diffusa* for most of the year. *Euphorbia nicaeensis* 'Blue Peaks' has grey-blue foliage and *Senecio serpens*, a succulent from South Africa, has foliage which is even more blue. One late afternoon the sky was bathed in a strange blue light which reflected into the sea, exactly the tone of the frosted shoots of the succulent senecio.

Artefacts in the garden also relate to the sea. A ceramic was created by Jenny Spiegal who lived on the Peninsula and captured the colours and movements of the water in the glaze. If you sit on the bench, you can look through the central hole in the ceramic to see the sea.

And I have palms. I indulged in palms: nikau from the Chathams, Great Barrier Island, Little Barrier and the Kermadecs grow with the little mountain palm and the big mountain palm from Lord Howe. Deep snow buried the South Seas Garden in August 2004. My palms, my treasured tender plants, how would they fare? It was days before the snow retreated but the palms popped out looking just as before. I am tickled pink by the palm trees. The textural plantings eddy and flow but they are just a homage to the beautiful view, and surrounding lyrical landscape, which engulfs the senses and bathes the soul.

OPPOSITE: *View across the South Seas Garden to the belvedere, showing the newly built stonework, just three years from planting.*

ABOVE: *The pageant of changing light seen from the viewing platform above the South Seas Garden. Taiaroa Heads, where albatrosses and penguins nest and breed, is in the distance and Harbour Cone, a distinctive peninsula landmark, is on the right.*

CHAPTER ELEVEN

Southern Plants from Southern Lands

New Zealand natives took London by storm at the 2004 Chelsea Flower Show. The sensational '100% Pure New Zealand Ora – Garden of Well Being' won a coveted Gold Medal and visitors queued for up to one and a half hours to view this garden composed solely of New Zealand native plants. Why was the garden so successful?

Sculptural plants in many shades of green and bronze contrasted sharply with the other multi-coloured floral garden exhibits. Kim Jarrett's design drew the spectator inwards, and its circles and coils differed markedly from the cubical structure of the show's other more traditional gardens. Trish Waugh's plantsmanship was exquisite; however, she paid tribute to the Maori sculptor Lyonel Grant whose work brought spiritual values to the garden which, she said, lifted it into another sphere.

Grant's carved *'kaitiaki'*, the guardians of sustainability, were enclosed by a verdant array of distinctively foliaged plants. The garden featured silica thermal terraces, a cavern where the spirits of the underworld dwelt, and a healing geothermal pool, or *'ngawha'*. Grant's sinuous carving of *Moko Waiwera* – the water lizard – was the garden's centrepeice. Ambient birdsong and the volcanic steam that wafted through the tree ferns, palms and cordylines all helped to create the distinctive atmosphere.

Red South African montbretia highlights New Zealand native plants, including kowhai, Pseudopanax laetus *and tree ferns in the Rainforest Garden.*

At Chelsea, I was proud to be in our New Zealand garden for some shifts, answering questions from the surging crowds. The two most asked about plants were *Pseudowintera colorata* 'Red Leopard', a burgundy-spotted horopito selected by Denis Hughes of Blue Mountain Nursery, and *Pseudopanax ferox*, which is sometimes called our fierce lancewood, with its long jagged leaves pointing downwards from a single stem.

New Zealand has a bold and rugged landscape which is lit by a bright clear light. Until the relatively recent arrival of mankind, most of the land was clothed in a verdant mantle of primeval forest. In the south, there were vast tracts of southern beech (*Nothofagus)*, stretching from deep valleys to the treeline. The light was filtered by the delicate tracery of millions of tiny leaves. Seedling trees and mosses carpeted the forest floor. Forests of hardwood podocarp trees grew on the west and northern coasts of the South Island and most of the North Island. The columnar trunks of the primitive podocarps rose like Doric columns through the broad-leafed trees. Their canopies, hung with epiphytes, overtopped the rest of the forest. Beneath were lianes, shrubs and layers of ferns. Kauri trees dominated the northernmost forests, and their great trunks were wide as well as tall. An early explorer mistook them for cliffs. Before grazing animals were introduced, these forests were impenetrably dense.

In coastal gullies were bold stands of nikau palms. Alien looking grass trees (*Dracophyllum* spp), with bunches of leaf blades at the ends of their branches, bore cream panicles of heath-like flowers. Metrosideros trees, pohutakawas in the north and ratas further south, flowered scarlet or crimson in summer. When mature, pohutakawas are usually wider than high, with rugged spreading limbs that are often hung with aerial roots which grow into the ground when a branch bends earthward.

The ginger-headed red tussock *(Chionochloa rubra)* marched across peat bogs like armies of trolls. Wind waves rippled the ash-blonde mountain tussock which covered vast high areas of the Southern Alps. Our flaxes (*Phormium*) and iconic cabbage trees (*Cordylines*) repeated the same thrusting leafy forms, and were a characteristic of open spaces. New Zealand plants have personality. Most are evergreens which have subtle seasonal changes, maintaining their integrity for twelve months of the year.

My family nurtured my interest in native plants. My mother grew them in our garden when I was a child, which was an unusual pastime in the 1940s and 1950s. I was brought up to be aware of and value 'the bush', New Zealanders' down-beat appellation for their native forests. Years ago, just before my aunt died, she said that there was a book for me on her kitchen table. It was *Our New Zealand Trees and Flowers* by E.C Richards, which was then just about the only book on our distinctive flora for the gardener or bushwalker.

I don't have a garden which only includes New Zealand native plants. I am too eclectic for that, with a passion to collect plants from all over the world. I can't stop myself. My acquisitive habits ensure there is a long line of plants in the shadehouse awaiting placement in the garden. In my garden of ideas,

OPPOSITE: *New Zealand's gold-medal-winning garden at the Chelsea Flower Show in 2004 featured our native plants. I spent time assisting and I'm shown here wearing the Tourism New Zealand uniform.*
ABOVE: *A bellbird feeds in our big rata tree. The blue on the bird's head is pollen from the native fuchsia which it must have just visited.*

ambience comes first and then I fit in the plants. I have integrated New Zealand plants throughout the gardens and grounds, valuing their structural qualities, individuality and connection to our land, in particular.

Within the area close to the Castle, which is laid out in the European landscaping tradition, native plants give a local twist. As the ephemeral flowering of exotics passes, the New Zealand designer plants remain as the stayers.

One day when I went to the shadehouse to pick up some conifers to use as 'dot' plants for a box parterre, I saw some Chatham Island flaxes and thought, 'Why not?'. I used them in the scheme instead of the more traditional choice. Elsewhere, Fiona has clipped the white-leafed *Pittosporum* 'Irene Patterson' and lophomyrtus into topiary balls. In the Rock Garden tapestry, I have orange leaves with orange flowers. Spikey *Libertia peregrinans* is filtered through polyanthus, crown imperials, the later geums and double Welsh poppies. The burgundy foliage of Cordlyline *'Red Fountain'*, which I have planted again – I love it – in a focal container in the rainforest, echoes red trillium petals and the plum-coloured leaves of *Saxifraga fortunei* 'Black Ruby'.

It is equally delicious with the summer fireworks of dahlias that emerge as the trilliums die down. *D.* 'Bishop of Llandaff,' the scarlet flowered old favourite since 1928, mingles with recent New Zealand

hybrids raised by Dr Keith Hammett, including the black-leafed, citron *D.* 'Golden Clarion' and crimson *D.* 'Ayrlies'. They all have vibrant single flowers shooting from dusky foliage. Beneath the weeping, fine-leafed stems of a rimu tree, I have planted blue on blue. Flowering rivers of filigree *Corydalis flexuosa* flow through boldly thrusting Chatham Island forget-me-nots. In the marble bath – it's such a spunky container – I have *Astelia chathamica* 'Silver Spear' with *Alstroemeria* 'Red Baron'.

I don't have a white garden. That has been done before. But among smokey-blue rhododendrons I do have white-flowered forms of the wood anemone *(Anemone nemerosa)*, bleeding heart *(Dicentra spectabilis)*, bergenias, fritillarias, meconopsis, the tall white *Thalictrum delavayi* for autumn and our own white Chatham Island forget-me-nots.

Tawny tussocks *(Carex comans)* are enlivened by interplantings of garnet, bell-like *Fritillaria pyrenaica*, with their throats of harvest-gold, moonlight trilliums, yellow hellebores and the new coloured-leafed *Heuchera* 'Amber Waves'. Dare I say that the carex look dingy without the flashes of colour?

However, some natives are the main event. The flamboyant kaka beak (*Clianthus*), is placed so that it can be viewed from below, as its flowers hang along the undersides of its branches. It prefers light soil

---

OPPOSITE, LEFT: *Warm-coloured flowers are enhanced by rich foliage.* Libertia peregrinans, *one of New Zealand's native irises, with polyanthus.* RIGHT: *A dark flax (*Phormium *'Platt's Black') with polyanthus.* ABOVE: *Primroses, cowslips and blue* Corydalis flexuosa *mingle with dwarf silver astelia* (Astelia nivicola).

with good drainage. The stunning Poor Knights lily (*Xeronema callistemon*) grows in scoria in its natural island home in the north of New Zealand. My containerised plant was placed at the foot of a north-facing wall beside the Dungeon. It used to be over-wintered in the glasshouse, as it was thought to be tender here, but one year I forgot to shift it and it didn't blink. So I have since planted some out in the garden, digging in coke breeze to help with drainage. A feed of Triabon helps my containerised plant have more than 40 flowers – not bad for Dunedin! Books describe the flowers as glistening scarlet bottlebrushes tipped with gold, but to me their curved stems seem shaped more like lavatory brushes.

I am growing a *Metrosideros parkinsonii* espaliered on a trellis because its scarlet rata flowers sprout from the woody branches. A self-sown native fuchsia tree (*Fuchsia exorticata*), left when we cleared away the second growth from the Rock Garden, is now fortuitously growing beside a little bridge at the back of the area. Long flakes of bark peel from its salmon-coloured, multi-stemmed silken trunk. Flowers open a Granny Smith-green colour, and then turn fuchsia with navy-blue pollen.

I continue to plant native trees, although not nearly enough, and they slowly grow. I hope others who may follow will do the same. Recently we have established a native plant trail that has been enthusiastically received by visitors.

Why were New Zealand plants distinctly different from those of the European countries our ancestors left to come to this newly settled land? The answer lies in our geological past, our long isolation and temperate climate. After the lost subcontinent Zealandia broke up, what is now New Zealand became isolated and was reshaped many times as land sank beneath the sea and mountain chains were thrust up by volcanoes and the collision of tectonic plates. Ice ages came and retreated. Over tens of millions of years through all these tumultuous events, there were always refuges for New Zealand's stock of primitive plants, little places that didn't sink or freeze.

As conditions for their welfare improved, plants repopulated emergent land. Because of these refuges our ancient plants survived, and 81 per cent are endemic – that is, naturally found nowhere else in the world. The history of our plants goes back even further, beyond Zealandia and into the deepest past.

OPPOSITE, TOP: *Donald and Douglas Larnach entertain their friends at Larnach Castle among the flax bushes and cabbage trees.* BELOW: *Kaka beak* (Clianthus maximus)
LEFT: *I am proud of this Poor Knights lily* (Xeronema callistemon). *It stays outside all year in a container even though it comes from an island off the coast of northern New Zealand.*
BELOW: *The peeling bark of the native fuchsia tree (*Fuchsia excorticata*), the biggest fuchsia in the world.*

Africa, Antarctica, South America, India, Australia and New Zealand were all joined 200 million years ago in one great southern continent called Gondwana. Over vast periods of time Gondwana broke up, and the continents segmented and drifted apart on the moving plates that formed the crust of the earth.

It was the great scientists Charles Darwin and Joseph Hooker who first observed and discussed the relationships of the floras of the southern lands. "Is not the similarity of the plants of Kerguelen's Land and South America very curious?" Darwin wrote to Hooker in 1843. Hooker agreed. "I do not know that there is in the north any instance of the floras of two such remote spots such as Kerg Land and Cape Horn being identical." Hooker asked, "How does it happen that *Edwardsia grandiflora* (now *Sophora*, or kowhai) inhabits both New Zealand and South America?"

At that time, these men, and others, had various theories, including the possibilities of chains of islands, or of seed travelling by sea or in the bellies of birds. Later scientists talked of land bridges and submerged continents. But it was Alfred Wegener, a German meteorologist, who in 1915 first propounded the theory of the drifting of the continents. He was to die in the field and was buried in the ice of Greenland long before his theories were taken seriously by more than a handful of geologists. It was as recently as 1956, at the Continental Drift Symposium in Hobart, that the theory gained mainstream scientific acceptance.

I decided to see for myself the relationships between the plants of old Gondwana. My search began with our southern beech trees, *Nothofagus*. My great grandparents had called their farm in the Canterbury foothills 'Birchlands' because they thought that the surrounding trees were birches. These trees were later classified as beeches. My desire to see the sisters of our beeches took me first to Tasmania. There the locally called myrtle, *Nothofagus cunninghamii*, grows in temperate rainforest. I also saw *N. gunii*, a small deciduous tree or bush, on Cradle Mountain.

Next I went to Chile which has nine or ten *Nothofagus* species, compared with five in New Zealand and three in Australia. They are the dominant trees of southern Chile. There I saw the magnificent evergreen *N. dombeyi* and the deciduous *N. obliqua*, which is referred to locally as roble, growing in fields, creating a park-like picture. Growing high in the Andes in scoria, *N. pumilio* is a reduced and dainty shrub. On Cerro La Campana I saw Chile's northernmost beech, *N. macrocarpa*, with a great horned owl sitting on one of its branches. By this tree was a bronze plaque set into rock commemorating 'Carlos Darwin', who had passed this way in 1834. I wondered what were his thoughts in this place at that time.

I went back to Australia, to Queensland, to find *N. moorei*, which is known locally as the Antarctic beech. It survives as a remnant population which has retreated to higher altitudes. I saw it in Lamington National Park growing at 942 metres. This tree, which will grow in New Zealand including Southland areas, has shiny leaves that are larger than those of other evergreen hardy *Nothofagus*, and new growth is an attractive dark red.

In New Caledonia, at 1,150 metres high on Mt Do, I saw *N. codonandra* with its large bullate leaves and bronze new growth. Here it grew with *Araucaria laubenfelsii*, *Metrosideris nitida*, *Dracophyllum ramosum*, *Podocarpus sylvestris* and *Ascarina rubricaulis*, which looked just like our own native hutu (*Ascarina lucida*), considered to be one of the most primitive of flowering plants. All of these belong to ancient Gondwana families. I was seeing again the combinations of plant families that

occur and reoccur around the South Pacific, with different species within these families in very different, widely separated lands. An abundance of *Nothofagus* pollen has been found in Antarctica, a reminder of trees that grew there when the continent enjoyed a warmer climate.

New Zealand's kauri (*Agathis australis*), a part of our national consciousness, is a member of the Araucariaceae family, which has an ancient lineage. Petrified araucaria have been found at Curio Bay in Southland. Fossilised remains of an ancestral kauri, *Agathis jurassica*, which date back to 175 million years ago, have been found at the Talbragar fish beds in New South Wales, Australia. Our kauri has sisters in Australia, New Caledonia and New Guinea. *Agathis robusta*, not as large as ours but a stately tree, grows in rainforests in Queensland. There I also saw *A. microstachya*, which is called the bull kauri because of its massive trunk. Most of the New Caledonian kauris are similar to ours but of less bulk and majesty. My favourite was *A. ovata*, the 'bonsai' kauri. Usually the leaves are glaucous and, unlike other kauris, it branches low and has a spreading habit. It grows in the cool mists of the mountains. Pin colonnaire (*Araucaria columnaris*), pencil thin but always with a bent trunk, grows to 60 metres by the golden sand of New Caledonia's tropical beaches.

OPPOSITE, TOP: *It was a thrill to find a plaque set into a rock face on La Campana in Chile commemorating Charles Darwin, who passed this way on his travels.* BELOW: *Chilean botanists stand below the plaque to Darwin.* ABOVE LEFT: *Pencil pine* (Athrotaxus cupressoides) *near Cradle Mountain in Tasmania.* RIGHT: Nothofagus codonandra *with a monkey puzzle tree relative,* Araucaria laubenfelsii, *on Mt Do in New Caledonia.*

My daughter Sophie, who accompanied me on my quest for araucaria in Australia, called *A. cunninghamii*, or hoop pine, the cheer-leader tree because the leaf-bearing stems are bunched at the ends of the branches like great pom-poms. In Queensland we saw stands of hoop pine in moister areas in Lamington National Park and many more on the Atherton Tableland. Our journey took us from Brisbane, through the Great Dividing Range and on to the Bunya Mountains. These rise quite steeply from a savannah-like plain to 1,000 metres. The bunya tree, *A. bidwillii*, spreads its great rounded crown over the rainforest. Its huge cones, weighing up to 10 kilograms, have large tasty nuts which are a traditional food of the Aborigines of Australia, as are the pehuen, or monkey puzzle tree nuts, food for the Araucarian Indians of South America.

I have a large monkey puzzle tree in the grounds at Larnach Castle and I wanted to see this tree growing in the wild. When in Chile we set up camp on the scoria among the monkey puzzle trees on the flanks of a living volcano. In this land of snow-capped active volcanoes, black rivers of scoria have destroyed all life in their paths. But then lichens, followed by beech and monkey puzzle trees reclaimed the fractured mountain slopes. Monkey puzzle trees live for a thousand years. We climbed the slopes of the Sierra Nevada to the summer snowline where dwarfed araucaria grew in the January snow. Bunya trees and monkey puzzles look like sisters, yet today they grow on lands so far apart. The bunya has affinities with *Araucaria mirabilis*, now only known from fossils found in Patagonia.

This tree grew 200 million years ago in a damp climate before the Andes had risen and created the rain shadow over the plains of Argentina to the east. The southern continents were rafted apart with their cargo of plants and are now separated by the South Pacific Ocean. Bunyas and monkey puzzle trees, the descendants of *A. mirabilis*, live on, little changed over hundreds of millions of years.

I went to New Zealand's subantarctic islands on the Russian Polar Research Vessel *Akademik Shokalskiy*. On Campbell Island, *Bulbinella rossii* grew huge and lush along with the megaherbs *Stilbocarpa polaris, Anisotome latifolia* and *Pleurophyllum speciosum*. Other bulbinella species are native to New Zealand and South Africa.

In both New Caledonia and the rainforests of Australia I have seen cordylines, sisters of our iconic

OPPOSITE, TOP: *We reboard the landing craft as we leave Enderby Island, one of the Auckland Islands group.* CENTRE: *I get up close to* Bulbinella rossii *on Campbell Island.* BELOW: *Monkey puzzle trees (*Araucaria araucana*) in the Chilean Andes.* THIS PAGE: *Some of the magnificent megaherbs growing on Campbell Island.* ABOVE: Pleurophyllum speciosum. RIGHT: Pleurophyllum criniferum *with* Bulbinella rossii. BELOW: Stilbocarpa polaris *which, to my delight, is now growing in my own garden.*

cabbage tree. Cordylines spread around the South Pacific islands but there is also a member of the family in Bolivia. Cordyline cousins, evolving from a common Gondwana ancestor, became the fucraea of South America, migrating north across the land bridge to become the agave of Mexico and the arid areas of the southern United States. In Australia, grass trees or black boys (*Xanthorrhoea* sp.) and lomandra evolved from this ancestor. The lomandras, botanically the closest of these to our cabbage tree, are rush-like plants in Australia. *Lomandra insularis*, which I saw in New Caledonia, formed a little trunk to nearly a metre. In South Africa, plants of this descent became aloes.

I found it fascinating that *Drimys winteri*, one of the earliest flowering plants to evolve, which I saw in the cloud forest above the desert in Northern Chile and again in Southern Chile, is closely related to *Drimys lanceolata* from Tasmania and our own horopito. Fossil pollen of other drimys are found in South Africa and Israel. Flamboyant proteas, the national flower of South Africa, and waratah, the national flower of New South Wales, the macadamia nut tree of Queensland Australia, the guevina nut from the forest of Chile and our own rewarewa are all members of Proteaceae, another primitive Gondwana plant family.

By the staircase in the South Seas Garden at Larnach Castle I had a – comparatively – hot spot. A rain shadow in the lee of the macrocarpa trees, it provided an opportunity to grow xerophytes, which is a flash word for plants that have adapted to growing in dry conditions. 'Out of Africa' is my name for this garden of aloes, restios and flamboyant gazanias. Our New Zealand bellbirds joyfully feed on the nectar of aloes, many of which flaunt their orange and yellow flowers in winter. There has been research done which shows that New Zealand birds prefer feeding on New Zealand native plants but this research has not been read by the bellbirds at Larnach Castle.

I have a drift of *Aloe polyphylla*, a fleshy, spiny-leafed chunky plant with growth spiralling out from the centre. You have to wait a year or two, with some tension and anticipation, to see whether each particular plant is going to spiral anticlockwise or clockwise. This aloe comes from the mountains of Lesotho and grows at 2,600 metres where there is a high precipitation, even snow in winter. Provided

it has perfect drainage, it is hardy in a temperate climate. I have planted the golden *Bulbinella setosa* from South Africa, which originates from an area that is winter wet and summer dry, so it is dormant in summer and emerges and flowers in winter. Its cousin, the similar *Bulbinella rossii*, from the subantarctic islands, rests in winter to emerge and flower in early summer. Are plants not clever in the way they adapt?

Fleshy aeoniums from the Canary Islands and massive agaves add their sculptural qualities to the xerophyte garden. On a ledge above 'Out of Africa' and the 'South Seas Garden', an aged *Cordyline australis*, our New Zealand cabbage tree, stands sentinel over its Gondwana relatives – lomandra from Australia, fucraea from South America, agaves from Central and North America and aloes from South Africa.

OPPOSITE, LEFT: Bulbinella setosa, *from South Africa, flowering in the Rock Garden.* RIGHT: *Chatham Island forget-me-not* (Myosotidium hortensia). ABOVE: Mitraria coccinea, *a scandent plant from Chile where it is pollinated by hummingbirds. It is another plant that provides food for our native bellbirds.*

CHAPTER TWELVE

Now This Is the Garden

At the entrance to the garden I painted a picture. I used plants and flowers for my palette and trees for a frame, but like a bold sculpture it has a third dimension which the visitor is invited to enter. It also has a fourth dimension – time. A garden is the interface between nature and art. It changes with the seasons and over the years, affirming life's processes of growth, death and renewal.

My entrance picture introduces themes which are further played out in the garden beyond. Grand old macrocarpa trees stand about as they do on the Otago Peninsula. Drystone walls, linking the rural countryside to the garden, lead to the gate. Snowdrops emerge soon

LEFT: *Hosta and* Astilbe *foliage grace the entrance with tree ferns* (Cyathea medullaris*) and flowering rhododendrons beyond.* ABOVE: *Drystone walls on the Otago Peninsula. Larnach helped his workers build walls on his property and we continue this wall-building process today.*

after the winter solstice, signalling the beginning of the floral procession that salutes the changing seasons. A succession of rhododendrons flower throughout the three months of spring in swathes of pink and white, with a few brave reds that bejewel the velvet lawn. In summer it is fluffy astilbes that flaunt their flowers, followed by Japanese anemones in autumn. There is a group of voluptuous tree ferns and I have planted New Zealand native trees including three kauri, which will one day make a statement. I wish they would hurry up and grow.

Rosette-leafed bridal wreath (*Francoa ramosa*), with long sprays of white flowers in late summer, is massed on the steep bank. I saw it growing wild in Chile below a plaque commemorating Charles Darwin. With them are *Celmisia mackaui,* a lush-leafed New Zealand daisy which grows this way on a bank by a stream near the sea on Banks Peninsula, and nikau palms which I saw there too. Young bunya trees are a reminder of our Gondwana connection. Our gem of a ticket office was designed by the celebrated architect Sir Miles Warren, perhaps his smallest commission, but significant as it suggests the colonial Castle which is partially glimpsed through the massive trees.

The garden is dominated by the Victorian Castle, its initial audacity now mellowed by time As just its present caretaker, I trod carefully when handling areas close to the historic buildings, respecting tradition, what had been done by others before me, and with an awareness that the Castle is a part

CLOCKWISE FROM LEFT: *Visitors enjoy the Serpentine Walk. Tree ferns and rhododendrons near the entrance gate. The gateman hands a visitor a garden map at the ticket office designed by Sir Miles Warren.* OPPOSITE, CLOCKWISE FROM TOP: *A fountain from Pisa in Italy plays on the Raised Lawn. Visitors walk down the Laburnum Pergola which turns gold in November. The Duchess from the drawing by Tenniel for* Alice's Adventures in Wonderland.

of many lives. But I was more spirited when I flung the garden out into the landscape.

We British settlers brought with us a long tradition of gardening stretching back more than 3000 years. It was in Egypt that the first people made gardens in what was to become the Western tradition, controlling the landscape and plants for aesthetics and pleasurable repose. Their gardens always had a central tank. Water was essential in the desert, without it there would be no life. The Persian word for garden is the same as their word for paradise. Their ancient gardens had the same central water pond, often with fountains, and were quartered by canals. Italians absorbed these traditions and built gardens to an axial plan, focused on their architecture. The British took on all these ideas and those of medieval monasteries and the broideries of the French. Then their own landscape movement cleared most of these fashions away. In the nineteenth century the British became plant collectors as a multifarious bounty was brought back from all around the world.

Traces of this long history of gardening mark my ground. Centrally placed at the front of the Castle is a round pond with a fountain symbolising the source of life. We keep the surrounding lawn as one great clear simple expanse, open to the sky, but the paths which once quartered this space can still be read as indented shadows on the lawn. A central axis from the Castle and through the garden thrusts into the landscape. Patterns in box and hedges define the designs. Woven into and around this structure is a comprehensive collection of plants arranged in changing pictures.

Drawing these elements together, I have created my own garden paradise.

Artefacts in the garden reflect the culture of the old world and the new. Mrs Purdie placed in the garden the figures of the Duchess and the Knave of Hearts from *Alice's Adventures in Wonderland*. This English book was a bestseller at the time that Larnach was building the Castle. When I needed ideas I read this book again, because didn't Alice fall down a rabbit hole thinking she would come out in the Antipathies?

We now have a door in a tree, the constantly photographed throne and a Cheshire cat in the cedar tree. We commissioned the cat to be carved from Oamaru stone and, expecting its imminent arrival, wrote in our new garden guide, "Can you find the Cheshire cat?" We started handing out this brochure but the cat was delayed, so many people were looking around the garden for a cat which was not yet there. Jim Morris was working in the grounds and he said, "It's a funny thing. I've been working here for 20 years and no one has ever asked me where the Cheshire cat is before, and three people asked me this morning."

In the South Seas Garden new drystone retaining walls have been recently built, echoing those made by the Scottish settlers on Otago Peninsula. Glen Coster, the stonemason, taught the apprentices

Alistair Collie and Louis Munro this traditional craft, keeping the skill alive A metal kete by the artist Joe Kake is installed in sight of the coastal inlets as a reminder of the first settlers, the Maori, who gathered shellfish there in their woven baskets. A car tyre is made into an urn in the Kiwi vernacular, as has graced many a seaside bach.

The spirit of the harbour and hills eddies around the garden, the vigorous landforms expressing their turbulent volcanic origin. I have addressed the landscape in the strength and scale of the garden. The surrounding scenery and pervading oceans are embraced in vistas and panoramas. An installation of igneous rock pays homage to what the peninsula is made up of. Oh, we've had fun.

It is with enormous gratitude that I look back on a lifetime's passion for plants. Curiosity about where they came from took me on voyages to islands, into forests and up mountains in our own and distant lands. What I saw in the field awakened my curiosity about plant distribution and the mysteries of evolution. I read voraciously, travelling a different journey, into the deeply distant past. I discovered that plants had inhabited the world for hundreds of millions of years before that outrageous weed, mankind, came along and shoved them aside. I learnt how mankind relies on plants because

---

OPPOSITE, TOP: *We commissioned this sculpture in Oamaru stone of the Cheshire cat. It grins down at visitors from the bough of a cedar tree.* OPPOSITE: *The succulent* Aeonium undulatum pseudo tabulaeform *flowers in the newly created rock fall.* Azorella trifurcata, *a Gondwana plant, grows around a stone seat.* ABOVE: Clematis *'Purity', a hybrid of New Zealand species cascades around the metal kete or basket. Maori once gathered shellfish in flax kete in the coastal bays below the South Seas Garden.*

we have not yet learnt to photosynthesise. Without plants there would be no birds, bees, animals, or you and me. Plants are our elders and I respect them.

A garden is a celebration of the natural world, the miracle of creation. Living plants are the subliminal keys to the present climate and the distant past, a connection to the land. But a garden is a human landscape, an art form of total immersion. Involved are the management of space, form and light to create a sequential experience. The visitor moves through from dark, enclosed detail to wide spaces open to the sky. It is an experience of the moment – a petal drops, the light changes, the garden moves on.

The garden at Larnach Castle is the sweep of my life. As a young girl I fell in love with a fairytale Castle and made the decision that looking after it and the surrounds would be my life's work. In the lost rock garden I discovered gardening, the joy of it and a wonder of plants. Into the garden I have poured all my memories, my shared Western culture, my creative aesthetic and my fascination with natural history. I have created a botanical theatre which I happily share. People come to play out their own celebrations. There are weddings and reunions and conferences, family outings, picnics on the lawn. Others, on a private odyssey are perhaps seeking in the garden a refreshment of spirit. I have been fortunate to have spent so much of my life doing what I love.

RIGHT: *A ceramic by Jenny Spiegal captures the colours and movement of sea and sky. It is surrounded by* Festuca coxii, *a blue-foliaged grass endemic to the Chatham Islands, and* Senecio serpens, *a succulent plant from South Africa.*

HOT TIPS

From the Gardeners at Larnach Castle

A garden is only as good as its maintenance and presentation on each particular day. We are mindful of visitors, and their time and money expended on the experience of the Larnach Castle garden. We enjoy the challenge to surprise and delight, it keeps us on our toes. In addition to the beautiful garden, we provide other necessities – clean toilets, on-site parking and food and drink in warm elegant surroundings. Visitors are supplied with interpretive leaflets.

What are my best tips? A wonderful team of gardeners, which we are fortunate to have, is required for a larger garden. They carry out sustained, thorough and sensitive maintenance. The garden at Larnach Castle is managed by head gardener Fiona Eadie, who has a BSc in

ABOVE: *Head gardener Fiona Eadie deadheads perennials in the Serpentine Walk.* RIGHT: *The castle and* Cyathea smithii *silhouetted against the sky, with* Cyathea dealbata, *New Zealand's national emblem, to the left. Both of these tree ferns are native to the Otago Peninsula.*

Botany from Otago University. Gary Drake maintains the lawns and paths. There are two apprentices, Alistair Collie and Louis Munro, to whom we pass on our accumulated experience, knowledge and skills as they tackle many different tasks. Andrea Shearer comes in to do deadheading and grooming. John Murray, the foreman, has contributed to the grounds over 26 years. Martin Eden, the plumber, who has been undergrounding and upgrading our services for four years, also turns the compost, shifts plants and soil and generally helps where the plumber's digger is required. Hard landscaping has mainly been done in-house but occasionally contractors have been used.

The secret of good husbandry lies with the soil which, in our garden on the top of a hill, is naturally thin and lacking in organic matter. We improve the soil continuously with compost and mulches of woodchips and pea straw. We mulch in winter when we have the time. Perennial plants have died and we mulch over them. Before mulching we remove any perennial weeds; annual weeds are smothered by the mulch. We cover the ground first with a couple of layers of newspaper, tucking it around the plants, then we place the pea straw or woodchips on top. Perennial plants come through this mulch but not seedlings of weeds or plants. The mulch physically protects and feeds the soil and plant roots, helps hold in moisture and reduces weeding chores to almost nil.

Compost is made in a row of four sheds with corrugated iron roofs, slatted wooden sides and earth floors. We are not scientific but just use what we have on this property and what is available nearby. Lawn clippings, garden refuse, kitchen waste and cardboard cartons are heaped in the first shed, just as they become available. Lime is added from time to time. When the heap is about two metres high, it is turned into the next shed and at this time it is mixed with a trailer-load of chicken manure. The chicken manure provides the nitrogen required by the microscopic organisms which break down the compost. At this stage the compost becomes hot, hopefully destroying any weed seeds or fungal diseases. We feel elated to see the compost steaming away. The compost is turned twice more into the third and fourth sheds. It is taken from the fourth shed for use in the garden.

We use fertilisers in the garden and on the lawn, because the soil is lacking certain nutrients. Lawn clippings are collected and composted because otherwise they would tramp into the house, so the nutrients that have been taken away are replaced. We now use coated, slow release fertilisers with micronutrients and trace elements. We have noticed a marked improvement in plant growth and health since using these modern fertilisers. Lawns are tipped frequently, never taking off more than a third, rather than 'cut short' and are scarified annually with a hired scarifier and sprayed biannually for weeds. Mowing patterns are changed so that the grass is encouraged to sit up.

We loosely run an integrated pest management system, relying on good observation within the garden and its surrounds, to catch any problems before they become serious. On spotting pests and diseases, we remove infected material and dispose of it off site if virulent. Our first method of control is maintaining good plant health with plenty of air movement. Prevention is the best means of cure – plants can look after themselves if they have the resources of good drainage and food in the soil.

Alas, box blight has visited our garden. Only a year after reading about this fungal disease (*Cylindrocladium buxicola*) infesting box plants in England, it was pointed out to me here by Rob Lucas, a gifted photographer and lecturer in horticulture at the Open Polytechnic of New Zealand, who was staying here as a guest for the Dunedin Rhododendron Festival. If there is a small infestation we take out the diseased box and put in new plants from a stock that we keep growing on. The hedges are sprayed with various fungicides using a pressure sprayer so that the chemical reaches into the centre of the plants; then they are fed to improve their health and resistance to disease. Reluctantly, we have decided to remove the 75-year-old box hedges behind the ballroom. To replace them, cuttings of *Coprosma propinqua* – found growing naturally on the property – have been taken by a nurseryman. The stock plant has small, light-green leaves and is well furnished to the base. We will monitor its progress and suitability for dwarf hedging.

Flowering plants are rigorously deadheaded for presentation and to redirect the energy of the plant. Instead of forming seed the plant is encouraged to use its resources for growth and flowering in the same or the next season. Hardy perennials, such as delphiniums

OPPOSITE: *Alistair Collie clips an arch in the macrocarpa hedge.* TOP: *Gary Drake edges the lawn with a line trimmer. This lawn has a riveted aluminium edge for the trimmer to cut against.* ABOVE: *Louis Munro uses a hired scarifier to dethatch the lawn. Alistair is raking up the thatch.*

and pyrethrum, are cut right to the ground and fed and they usually flower again later in the season. Half-hardy perennials and sub-shrubs such as wallflowers and penstemons are just shortened back. Flower heads of rhododendrons and azaleas are snapped off, taking care not to damage the growth buds which are just below the flower.

Foliage plants such as flax have old, scruffy leaves removed and shrubs have dead or unhealthy wood taken out as an ongoing process. Plants are pruned or clipped for shape. We have our mounds and balls but other shrubs are pruned and thinned to reveal their essential structure. We even prune rhododendrons if they are not doing what we want. We prefer not to let our shrubs develop into lumps, to jostle each other or overwhelm the under-planting. Woody plants are managed to reveal character or gracefulness and style. Contract arborists attend to and shape the trees. Presentation of the garden requires a good eye, not just when it is planted out, but in its care and maintenance.

We desperately avoid letting weeds seed. If we are short of time, an area is gone over to remove any seeding weeds first, then gone back over to finish the weeding and grooming. Fiona and I wear what my children call a 'bat belt', because Batman wears something similar. He probably doesn't carry in its pockets the same bits that we do. Fiona carries grape pruners, a Stanley knife and a small folding saw. I carry secateurs, a waterproof notebook and pencil to note down jobs that I see that need doing, and my secret weapon, a pot of poison and paintbrush. This is a little bottle of glyphosate (Roundup or G360) mixed with one-part water and one-part codacide or wetting agent. I paint this mixture onto weeds or creepers which are growing through plants, perhaps using newspaper to catch any drips, or onto weeds in close confines with precious plants where spray drift would be damaging. We have killed ivy in a holly hedge and running grass from a box hedge by this method. Keeping them in the pockets of our bat belts ensures that we do not lose our little tools.

The garden is constantly under review. We further refine the plantings visually or horticulturally,

ABOVE: *Nathan Kelly clips the box hedge. Powered hedge cutters are used but the final grooming is done by hand.* OPPOSITE, ABOVE: *My 'bat belt' showing secateurs, brush and a jar of weedkiller (glyphosate). Alistair checks the batter of the macrocarpa hedge.*

as we come to understand more closely the varying microclimates. The balance may have changed. If areas become tired, overgrown or just plain boring we are not afraid to pull out a whole lot of stuff. It gives us an opportunity to try something new. We think it more important to make the garden better rather than to make it bigger, except for planting trees in the landscape; a truly noble pastime. If a shrub is looking poorly and is not responding to treatment, we pull it out and start it off again with a young plant in a different place.

We don't hang on to it like you would to an old dog. An underplanting may be tired. We might dig it out and renew the soil, divide the plants and put them back, or better still, try something else to vary the look. It can be that a whole area needs change. We study it carefully, and decide what plants are have character or make a point, and drastically remove everything else. That's loads of fun, because then we can make a fresh new garden, the few remaining plants of maturity lending their personality.

The gardener walks with nature, hand in hand, but the life of nature is change. To manage and present is the work of the gardener.

Visiting Larnach Castle

Larnach Castle Garden
Larnach Castle Garden is open daily from 9 am to 5 pm. Extended hours during summer. The Ballroom Café is open daily from 9.30 am to 4.30 pm except Christmas Day.

Larnach Castle
Discover New Zealand's only Castle, built from 1871 and still privately owned and cared for by the Barker family. Larnach Castle features magnificent architecture, superb craftsmanship and New Zealand period furniture. Open daily except Christmas Day from 9 am to 5 pm.

Larnach Lodge
New re-creation of colonial farm building set in Larnach Castle Garden. Twelve individually themed rooms, all with private facilities. Breakfast served in the Stable.

Larnach Stable Stay
Six bedrooms with shared bathrooms in converted historic Coach House. Lodge and Stable Stay guests may dine in Castle dining room if booked by 5 pm.

Contact Details
145 Camp Road, Otago Peninsula, PO Box 1350, Dunedin.
Phone +64 3 476 1616; Fax +64 3 476 1574
Email larnach@larnachcastle.co.nz website www.larnachcastle.co.nz

Visiting Otago Peninsula

Larnach Castle Margaret Barker's garden at Larnach Castle is situated near Dunedin on the Otago Peninsula, which is renowned for its unique wildlife attractions. www.larnachcastle.co.nz

Royal Albatross Colony The world's only mainland breeding colony of these magnificent birds. www.albatross.org.nz

Penguin Place The world's rarest penguin, the yellow-eyed penguin, can be viewed from tunnels and hides at this conservation reserve. www.penguin-place.co.nz

Nature's Wonders Naturally A wildlife adventure aboard all-terrain Argo vehicles to view seals, penguins and cormorants. www.natureswondersnaturally.com

Monarch Wildlife Cruises View the peninsula wildlife from the Otago Harbour. www.wildlife.co.nz

Otago Peninsula www.otago-peninsula.co.nz

Tourism Dunedin www.dunedinnz.com www.cityofdunedin.com

Tourism New Zealand www.newzealand.com

New Zealand Gardens Trust Assessed gardens open to visit. www.gardens.org.nz

---

OPPOSITE: *The structure of the garden is etched in snow.*

TOP: *Otago Peninsula swathed in mist with just Harbour Cone visible from the South Seas Garden.*

Selected Bibliography

Adams, B. *The Flowering of the Pacific*. Sydney: William Collins Pty Ltd, 1986.

Boyer, K. *Palms and Cycads Beyond the Tropics*. Pub. Fund, Palm and Cycad Soc. of Australia, 1999.

Brickell, C. Ed. *RHS A–Z Encyclopedia of Garden Plants*. London: Dorling Kindersley Ltd, 1997.

Morris, R. and A. Ballance. *Island Magic, Wildlife of the South Seas*. Auckland: David Bateman Ltd, 2003.

Poole, A.L., *Southern Beeches*. NZ Department of Scientific and Industrial Research Information, Series No. 162, 1987.

Salmon, J.T. *The Native Trees of New Zealand*. Wellington: A.H. & A.W. Reed, 1980.

Simpson, P. *Dancing Leaves*. Christchurch: Canterbury University Press, 2000.

Stevens, G., M. McGlone and B McCulloch. *Prehistoric New Zealand*. Auckland: Reed, 1995.

White, M.E. *The Greening of Gondwana*. East Roseville: Kangaroo Press, 1998.

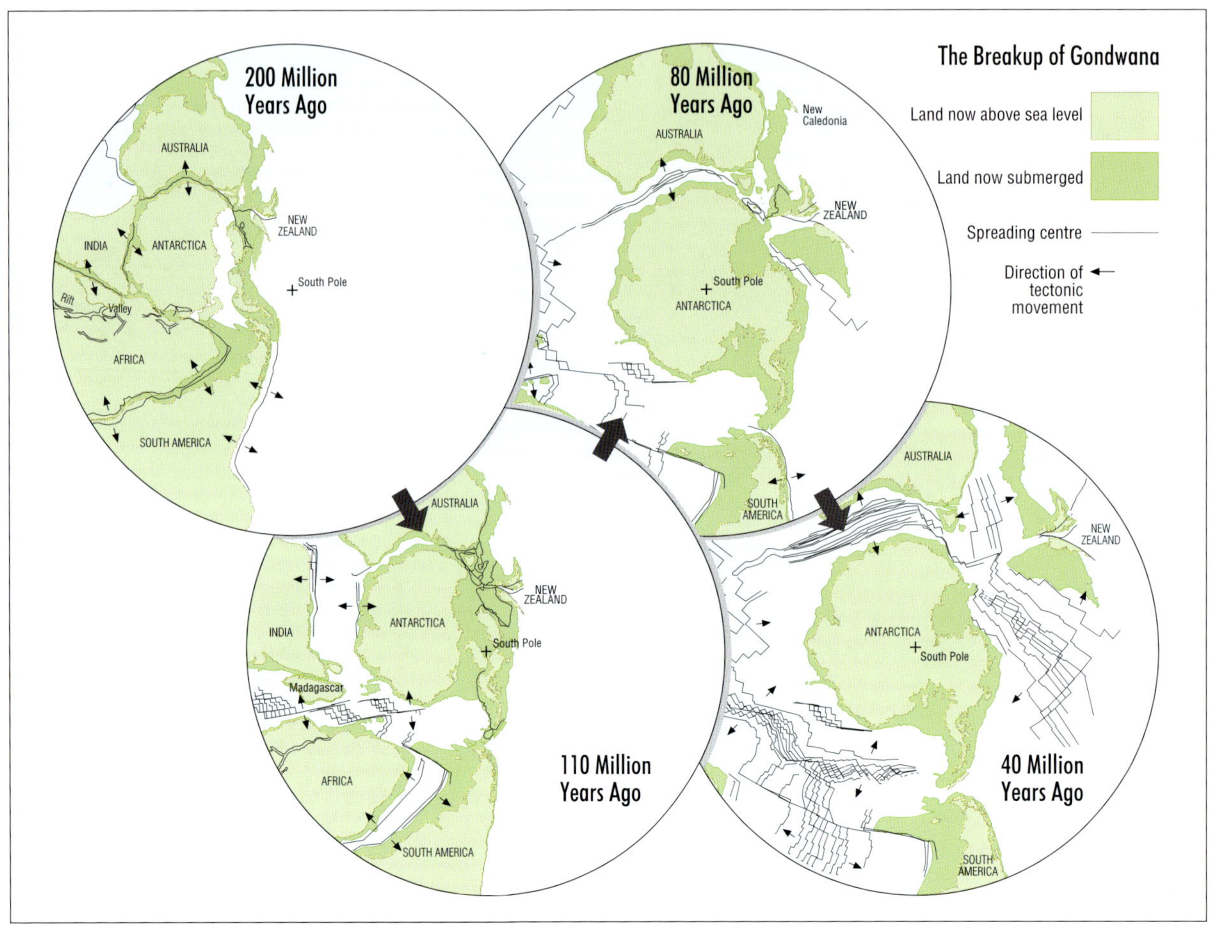

ABOVE: *Map showing breakup of Gondwana.*

OPPOSITE: *Avenue of New Zealand mountain cabbage trees (*Cordyline indivisa*).*

Photographic Credits

A. Apse 8/9; 33, top
Allied Press 34, top; 102
B. Barker 18, top and centre; 19, top, centre and lower; 28; 29; 30; 32; 33, lower; 34, lower; 37, top, centre left, centre right and lower; 40, top and lower; 48, lower; 58; 60; 63, centre; 82; 83, lower; 94, top and centre
M. Barker 7; 38/39; 45; 46, top; 47, top; 52, centre and lower; 56, top and centre; 57, left and right; 64; 68, top and lower; 77; 78; 79; 84; 88; 89; 93, top, centre and lower; 95, lower; 97; 98, top; 105; 106, top and centre; 107, lower; 108; 109; 111; 118, top; 120; 125; 134, top and lower; 135, left and right; 136, top and lower; 137, top left, right and lower; 138, left; 142, top right; 143, lower left; 144, lower; 151, lower
N. Barker 116, top and lower
S. Barker 95, top
Burton Bros. 23, centre
Moira Clark 100
M.L. Cox 92
J. Dawber 10; 43; 98, lower; 99; 118, lower; 119; 121; 141; 145; 148
G. Hanly 14/15; 42; 48, top; 49; 53; 72; 85; 86; 96, top; 104; 110; 112; 117; 122; 124; 138, right; 140/141; 144, top; 148/149; 157
S. Jaquiery 3; 4/5; 27; 35; 36; 41; 44, left and right; 55; 59; 67; 69; 70; 73; 75; 83, top; 90; 96, centre; 114; 126/127; 129; 130, left and right; 132, lower; 133, top and lower; 139; 142, left and centre; 143, top and lower right; 146/147; 150; 151, top; 152; 153, top and lower; 154; 160
D. King 40, centre
Larnach Castle Collection 16; 22, top; lower; 23, lower; 24; 26; 39; 61; 63, top; 132, top
L. McLeod 50/51; 102/103
J. Murray 25; 46, lower; 66; 87; 115; 131; 155
J. Nicholas 80/81
S. Preston 107, top
D. Raffills 47, lower
D. Sheratt 76
S. Tagg 65
Tourism Dunedin 101
A. Trott 128

Index

Acer shirasawanum 'Aureum' 3
Aciphylla glaucescens **112**
Aeonium spp 139, **144**
Allen, Fleur (Larnach descendant) **74**
Allen, Nicholas (Larnach descendant) **74**
Aloe polyphylla **119**, 138
Anemone pavonina **43**
Ansin, Ray (sculptor and designer) 55, 100
Araucaria spp 85, 122, 134, **135**, 136
A. araucana 23, **136**
A. bidwillii 136, 142
A. columnaris 122, 123, 124, 135
A. heterophylla 122, 124
Araucariaceae, see also kauri 122, 135
architects, Castle 22; ballroom 69; ticket office 142
Asphodelus albus **39**
Astelia chathamica 'Silver Spear' **59**, 120
A. nivicola 47, **131**
Asteranthera ovata **79**
Athrotaxus cupressoides **135**
Australia 22, 76, 134, **135**, **136**, 138
azaleas **9**, **65**, **66**, **67**, 68, 152
Azorella trifurcata **144**
ballroom 60–69, **83**
Banks, Rosamund 78
Barker, Barry 17, **19**, 30, **31**, 54, 64, 66
Barker, Charlotte **10**, **160**
Barker, Norcombe **10**, **29**, **31**, **37**, 57, **58**, **68**, **74**, 84, 93, **95**, 96, 97, 98
Barker, Sophie **10**, **28**, **29**, **31**, **37**, **40**, **48**, 57, **69**, **74**, 84, 93, 95, 98, 123, 136
beech, Southern Hemisphere, see *Nothofagus;* Northern Hemisphere, see *Fagus*
belvedere 114, **115**
Beschorneria yuccoides **112**
Blandfordia punicea **38**, **44**
blue poppies **72**, 82
box **15**, 23, 26, 58, **65**, 68, 84, 151, **152**
Brickell, Christopher 123
Bulbinella spp 122, **136**, **137**, **138**, 139
bunya 136, 142
Buxus spp **15**, 23, 58, **65**, 68, 84, 151, **152**
cabbage tree, see *Cordyline*
Cardiocrinum giganteum **81**, 88
cedars 54
Celmisia spp **46**, 87, 142
Chatham Island forget-me-not 119, 131, **138**
Chatham Islands 112-125
Chelsea Flower Show 126
Chiastophyllum oppositifolium **38**
Chile 74, 76, 88, **134**, **136**
Chilean fire bush 55
China 102-111
Chionochloa rubra (red tussock) **57**, 129
Cineraria candicans 76
Clematis spp 52, 54, **145**
Clianthus spp **114**, 131, **132**
Colchicum speciosum 67
Collier, Gordon (NZ plantsman) 79, 118
composting 41, 53, 150
Cordyalis flexuosa **131**
Cordyline 136
C. australis **7**, 23, **70**, 129, **132**
C. indivisa **86**, **157**
C. 'Red Fountain' **43**, **45**, 58
Cox, Kenneth 80, 108, 109
Cox, Peter 80, 108
Coxella dieffenbachii **119**
crown imperial **44**, 67, 68
Cupola **15**, 26, **27**
Cupressus macrocarpa 23, 27, **61**, 76, **98**, **118**, 141
Cyathea spp 85, **87**
Dahlia spp 53, 57, 130
Darwin, Charles 133, 134
Delphinium spp **56**, 151
Dicksonia spp 84, 85
Dillon, Helen 78, 116
Diplarrhena moraea **47**
Drimys winteri 78, 138
Dunedin Garden Botanic Garden 102
dungeon **29**
Eadie, Fiona (Castle employee) 68, 125, 130, 148
Empson, Oscar (previous owner) 17, 18
erica **65**, 68
Eucryphia cordifolia 79, **149**
Euphorbia polychroma **43**
Fagus spp **70**, **72**, **73**, 75
Festuca coxii **147**
Fitzroya cupressoides 79
flax, New Zealand, see *Phormium*
fountain **26**, **143**
France 91, 100
Fritillaria imperialis **44**, 67, 68
Fuchsia spp 79, 129, 132, **133**
Galtonia viridiflora **45**, 57
garden, maintenance 41, 53, 54, 58
Gazania sp **119**
Geranium maderense 52
Gladiolis papilio **64**
Glenfalloch (Dunedin garden) 102
golden rod (*Solidago*) **57**
Gondwana 82, 133, 134, 138, **156**
gossamer grass (*Anemanthele lessoniana*) **57**
Green Room **99**, **100**
Griselinia spp 79, 84, **85**
grounds employees, contractors 36, **37**, **68**, 69, 75, **95**, 96, 97, **100**, **116**, 124, 144, 148-153
Guest, Jim (lawyer) 95, 97
Gunnera spp 79
heather **65**, 68
Hebe spp 66, 68
hedges **53**, 58, **65**, 66, 68, 94, 98, 100, 151, **150**, **153**
Hidcote 56
Higgie, Clive and Nicki (Paloma garden, NZ) 48
holly 23, 27, **53**
Hooker, Joseph 133
Hosta spp **140**
Hydrangea actea 53
Inverewe 87
kahikatea (see also podocarps) 82

kaka beak **114**, 131, **132**
kauri (see also Araucariaceae) 85, 122, 128, 135
kowhai 122, **127**, 133
labernum **90,** 96, **101**
lancewood **117**, 120
Larnach, William 20–27, 32, 33, 34, 61, 62, 83, 84, 85, 141
Libertia peregrinans **130**
Lijiang, China 106
lily, giant **81**, 88
Lobelia tupa 88, **89**
Lodge **103**
lonicera 94
Lord Howe Island 122, 123, 125
Lost Rock Garden 38-49, **130**, **131**, **138**
McConnell, Beverley (Ayrlies garden, NZ) 54
macrocarpa, see *Cupressus macrocarpa*
marble bath 57, **58, 59**
Meconopsis betonicifolia **72**, 82
Methane Plant/gas 24, **25**,
Metrosideros 122, 123, 128, 132, 134
M. carminea **84**, 87
M. robusta **129**
Mitraria coccinea 79, **139**
monkey puzzle 23, **136**
montbretia **127**
Morris, Heather (Castle employee) 34
Morris, Jim (Castle employee) 31, 37, 54, **82**, 144
Morris, Sam (Castle employee) 37
Mount Cook lily **42**, 48
Murray, John (Castle staff) 54, 57, **58**, 64, 96, 114, 116, 150
New Caledonia 122, 134, **135**, 136
nikau palm, see *Rhopalostylis*
Nomocharis **47**, **109**, 110
Norfolk Island pine 122, 124
Nothofagus 128, 134, **135**
N. alpina 75
N. antarctica 75
N. obliqua 75, 134
N. fusca **81,** 84
Olearia spp 45, 119, 120
Onopordon acanthium **56**
Otago Alpine Garden Group 42
Otago Peninsula, climate 53, 76, 82, 113; general **33**, 96, 124, **125**, **155;** geology 22, 113; history 20, **21,** 22, 47, 82, 113; Taiaroa Head 32, 113, 124, **125**; vegetation 22, 82, 85
Ourisia spp 87
owners, previous (see also, Larnach, Empson, Purdie) 25, 27, 61
palms (see also *Rhopalostylis*) 76, 123, 125
pergola **90,** 93, 96, **98**
Phormium spp 52, 58, **119**, 129, **132**, 152
P. 'Platts Black' **130**
pin colonnaire 122, 123, 124, 135
pingao (NZ coastal 'grass') **122**, 124
plant care (see also pruning) 41, 53, 57, 68, 88, 119, 148-153
Pleurophyllum spp **137**
podocarps 23, **66**, **67**, 76, 82, **83**, 85, 88, 128, 134
ponds 26, 92, **93**, **95**, 96, **99**, **100**, 143
Poor Knights lily 132, **133**
pruning 54, 58, 67, 76, 95, 152
Pseudopanax spp **117**, 120, **127**
Pukeiti, NZ garden 79
Purdie, Mr J. Jackson (previous owner) 25, 26, 34, 39, 63
Purdie, Mrs Laura (previous owner) 25, 26, 32, 33, 34, 62, 144
puya 76, 78
Rainforest Garden 80-89, **111**, **127**, **139**, **149**
Raised Lawn **26**, **98**
Ranunculus lyallii **42**, 48
rata, see *Metrosideros*
rhododendrons 27, **43**, 63, 88, 102-111, **142**, 152
Rhododendron 'Cornubia' **111**
R. decorum **107**
R. edgeworthii 110, 111
R. grande **102**
R. 'Ilam Cream' 108
R. lacteum **108**, 109
R. maddenii ssp *maddenii* **85**
Rhopalostylis 85, **120**, 121, 125, 128
rimu, see also podocarps 23, 76, 82, **83**, **85**
Rock Garden, see Lost Rock Garden
roses 23, 52, 54, 71, 72
Scotch thistle **56**
Scotland 80, 87
Scottish Rock Garden Club 42
Senecio serpens **147**
Serpentine Walk 50-59, 142
shelter 23, 52, 73, 76, 96
Sissinghurst 56, 71, 72, 78
Smith, William Tayler (great-grandfather) 26
Snedden, Fleur (Larnach descendant) **74**
Snedden, Jim **74**
snowdrops 40, **41**, 57, 141
Sophora spp 55, 122, **127**, 133
South Seas Garden **102**, 112-125, 138, **144**, **145**, **146**
spiral aloe **119**, 138
Stable 23, 27, **72**
Stilbocarpa polaris 48, **137**
Subantarctic Islands 122, **136**, **137**
Taiaroa Head, see Otago Peninsula
Thalictrum delavayi 'Hewitts Double' **64**, 67
Thornicroft, Ira (Purdie contractor) 39
Ticket office **142**
totara (see also podocarps) 23, **66**, **67**, 83
Touchwood Books 72
Tourist Industry Association 18
Travel and Holidays Association 18
tree ferns (see also *Cyathea* and *Dicksonia*) **81**, 82, **84**, 123, **127**
Tresco 119
Trillium 47, 57, **59**
Tropaeolum polyphyllum **78**
Veratrum nigrum **88**
vinery **29**
Viola 'All Black' **43**
walls, drystone 23, **125**, **141**, 144
White, Cedric (father) **18, 28**, 40, 85, 91
White, Helen (mother) 18, **28**, 32, 40, 85, 91, 129
Wilmans (local family) 37, 57
Wishing Well **29**, 33
Xeronema callistemon 132, **133**
yew 64, 68, **95**, **97**, 100
Yunnan, China 105, **106**, **107**, **108**
Zealandia 121, 132

There are fairies at the bottom of the garden. My granddaughter Charlotte, holding wand, with her friend Kezia. Another generation of children enjoys playing in the garden at Larnach Castle.